D1448271

A Collector's Dictionary

HENRY HAINWORTH

Routledge & Kegan Paul

London, Boston and Henley

First published in 1981
by Routledge & Kegan Paul Ltd
39 Store Street, London WC1E 7DD
9 Park Street, Boston, Mass. 02108, USA and
Broadway House, Newtown Road
Henley-on-Thames, Oxon RG9 1EN

Set in 10/12 Linocomp Palatino by
Rowland Phototypesetting Ltd, Bury St Edmunds, Suffolk
and printed in Great Britain by
Whitstable Litho Ltd, Whitstable, Kent

British Library Cataloguing in Publication Data

Hainworth, Henry
   A collector's dictionary.
   1. Antiques – Terminology
   I. Title
   745.1'075   NK1110

   ISBN 0 7100 0745 0
   ISBN 0 7100 0511 3 Pbk

Contents

Tables

Introduction

This is a book about words – the specialized words used by collectors – but assembled and described in a personal way.

In the last decade there has been a great resurgence of interest in art and artefacts. This goes beyond material interest in acquisition for investment – though that element is there – and this wide appreciation of the products of human skill and ingenuity is always a matter for rejoicing since it bespeaks a corresponding intellectual curiosity that contradicts accusations of a wholly materialist evolution of society.

In response to this surge of interest there has appeared a steady stream of specialized books produced for enthusiasts and collectors, expert and amateur alike. Some of these books themselves are works of art of printer and publisher. They have been matched by a torrent of articles in publications ranging from the newspaper to the specialist journal, and by discourses and demonstrations on radio and television.

In every craft there grows up a specialized vocabulary where words in daily use have special meaning, or where special words are used which are not of daily currency. Of course, anyone who has enough specialist books or dictionaries can consult the appropriate one and learn the meaning of a term that seems obscure. But there seems to be a place for a collective glossary of the special words used in connection with the commoner arts and crafts and this volume is an attempt to fill that place. It is designed to be more convenient than a collection of specialist works on each of the subjects it attempts to cover, and may even provide some protection to the less initiated from an experienced salesman who seeks to enhance his prices by discharging a stream of 'specialized' jargon.

The book is put together on a grouping principle. In the present context this means that words or terms having relation to each other are brought together for comparative purposes. This system makes frequent cross-referencing necessary, and consequently a greater turning of the pages than is conventionally to be expected. But it is hoped that the enthusiast will agree that the placing of a word in the setting of its own 'family' is sufficient reward for the slight extra effort.

Every specialized term has its own alphabetic place in the dictionary, but often it is followed by no more than the cross-referencing symbol⟶ and another word. Further, any explanation that includes a **WORD** in capital letters means that further information is available under the entry for that **WORD**. Ordinary words that retain their ordinary dictionary meaning are generally omitted.

Proper names have created quite a problem. To list all the great creators and artists would make this catalogue quite unmanageable. Those sufficiently interested in the subject will not need an explanation of Rembrandt, Hester Bateman, Kändler, or Fabergé. Other and specialized books abound. Therefore only those persons or places are included which have given their names to an object, an epoch, or a style, now standing in its own right. In this one cannot hope to do justice to all; but one can at least hope to provoke the argument of the learned. The names of the Chinese dynasties are a special case – they are a form of dating and of style, and thus have their own special entries.

Likewise, foreign words have provoked their own peculiar problems. As the artefacts of other countries, deriving often from a unique cultural environment, have become in succession the objects of cupidity, possession, and collection, their native names have passed into daily usage among the Anglo-Saxon cognoscenti. The problem has been to know whether these words are admitted as fully English. There is no sure answer, and it has seemed right to include them, in italics where the respectable learned paper would still italicize them, and in ordinary print, as already assimilated, in other cases. The choice is subjective; and, fortunately, it is almost impossible to adjudicate. For if there is one single thing of which those of English tongue have been collectors, it is the words of others. The fact that in the take-over the word was sometimes grotesquely distorted, whether in meaning or pronunciation, is usually, in time, forgiven.

Dictionary

ACANTHUS   A (Mediterranean) plant, stylized representations of whose leaves are much used for decorative effect,
e.g. in the capitals of **CORINTHIAN** columns.

ADDORSED   Back to back.

AEOLOPILE (AEOLIPYLE)   An ancient instrument to demon-
strate the force with which the vapour generated by heat
in a closed vessel rushes out through a small hole in the
vessel.

AGATE   (1) ⟶ **STONES**
    (2) ⟶ **TYPE SIZES** (Table VI)

AIRTWIST   Of the stem of a wine-glass having a spirally twisting thread of air running from top to bottom.

À JOUR   Open, like lace.

ALABASTER   ⟶ **STONES**

ALB   ⟶ **VESTMENT**

ALEXANDRITE   ⟶ **STONES**

ALKALINE GLAZE   ⟶ **CERAMICS**

ALLOY   A mixture of metals, particularly of the rarer or more
expensive with a proportion of a cheaper metal or metals, in
order to reduce the price of the result. Alloying, however, is
also carried out to impart additional qualities, for example
hardness or ductility, to a rarer metal.

> **BRASS**   Historically an alloy of copper with tin, zinc, or
> other base metal, it is now generally two-thirds copper
> and one-third zinc. Yellow in colour.
>
> **BRITANNIA METAL**   A silver-coloured alloy of tin and
> **REGULUS** of antimony.
>
> **BRONZE**   An alloy of copper and tin, in the approximate
> proportion of 8 to 1. Brown in colour.
>
> **ELECTRUM**   (1) A natural gold ore containing from 20 to 50
> per cent silver.

(2) An alloy of copper, zinc, and nickel (cf. **GERMAN SILVER**).

GERMAN SILVER   A white alloy of nickel, zinc, and copper.

GOLD   It may seem strange to find so 'pure' a metal as we tend to think **GOLD** (or **SILVER**) figuring in a list of alloys. But the pure yellow metal gold is too soft for many purposes. Pure gold is so malleable that it can be beaten into leaves about one two hundred thousandth of an inch in thickness. In order to harden it, it is generally alloyed, principally with copper, for jewellery or other artistic uses, the proportion of pure gold in the alloy being measured in **CARATS**. $\longrightarrow$ **HALLMARK**

LATTEN   Now an archaic word – a yellow alloy similar to, or the same as, **BRASS**.

NIELLO   A black alloy of sulphur, lead, silver, and copper, used to fill engraving in silver and heighten the contrast.

ORMOLU   Originally gold or gold leaf ground and prepared for gilding brass, bronze, etc; hence gilded bronze used in the decoration of furniture. Now an alloy of copper, zinc, and tin, having the colour of gold and the great merit, characteristic of gold, and unlike brass, of virtually not tarnishing. This, indeed, was the original purpose of gilding brass or bronze, to have the untarnished effect of gold at a fraction of the price.

PAKTONG   An alloy of copper, nickel, and zinc imported into England from China in the second half of the eighteenth century and used in the manufacture of candlesticks, grates, and fenders (cf. **GERMAN SILVER**).

PEWTER   An alloy of tin and lead (or other metal). Grey in colour.

PINCHBECK   Alloy of copper and zinc, of golden colour, used as a substitute for gold in cheap jewellery. Its name comes from its discoverer, C. Pinchbeck, a watchmaker who died in 1732.

PLATINUM   A relatively rare, and therefore precious, white metal, like silver but less bright, very heavy, used chiefly for scientific and industrial purposes, but also in jewellery. In England platinum has, unlike gold and silver, had no legally prescribed standard of purity and no **HALLMARK**. But on the entry into force of the Hallmarking Act 1973 an alloy exposed for sale as platinum must be of a minimum standard of purity of 950 parts in 1000 (950 millesimes) and must bear the **HALLMARK** of an orb surmounted by a cross.

SHAKUDO   An alloy used in Japanese precious metal work and consisting of copper with 3 to 6 per cent of gold in it.

SHIBUICHI   An alloy used in Japanese precious metal work, consisting of 1 part silver to 3 parts copper, and grey in colour.

SILVER   Like **GOLD**, alloyed, generally with copper, for the creation of artefacts. The standard of measurement is expressed by the percentage of pure silver in the alloy. In Britain silver may not be sold below the **STERLING** standard (92.5 per cent pure silver). Goods are also, more rarely, manufactured of '**BRITANNIA**' standard (95.84 per cent). In Europe much silver is manufactured to a standard of 80 per cent purity, and in the Far East lower qualities are used. ⟶ **HALLMARK**

TUTENAG   This is not an alloy but is mentioned here as it is sometimes confused with **PAKTONG**. Tutenag is a zinc oxide that was formed in Chinese zinc smelting furnaces (often from zinc exported from England in the eighteenth century) and imported to England for polishing purposes.

WHITE GOLD   Although in the pure state a yellow metal, **GOLD** can be alloyed to a white or silver colour by a suitable choice of the alloying metals. As it is, however, recognized as gold, and can be so hallmarked, it must contain the percentage of yellow gold prescribed for its particular **CARAT** value. The whitish colour is obtained from a mixture of varying proportions of silver, copper, zinc, and nickel.

ALMANDINE GARNET   ⟶ **STONES**

ALTO RELIEVO/RILIEVO ⟶ RELIEF

AMARANTH, AMARANT   An imaginary flower that never fades.

AMBER ⟶ STONES

AMBRY (AUMBRY)   A cupboard or locker; a locker or recess in a church wall for holding sacramental vessels.

AMETHYST ⟶ STONES

AMORINO (pl. AMORINI)   Cupid⟶ PUTTO

AMPHORA   A tall two-handled vessel, usually of earthenware, for holding wine, oil, etc.

AN ⟶ CHINESE TERMS

ANDIRON   One of a pair of horizontal iron bars, held on two short pillars, usually ornamental in front, placed at each side of hearth to support burning logs; same as FIRE-DOG.

ANTHEMION   Stylized ornament based on the flower and foliage of the honeysuckle.

ANTIQUARIAN   Paper size⟶ Table I

APOSTLE SPOON   One whose handle ends in a figure of an apostle.

APOTHECARIES' WEIGHT ⟶ WEIGHTS (Table VII)

AQUAMARINE ⟶ STONES

AQUATINT ⟶ PRINT

ARABESQUE   Decoration in the form of flowing lines of branches, leaves, and scrolling, usually symmetrical.

ARCHITRAVE   Moulding round door frames.

ARGENT ⟶ HERALDIC TERMS

ARGYLL (ARGYLE)   Named after its reputed inventor, the fourth Duke of Argyll, a spouted vessel like a tea or coffee pot, for keeping gravy hot, by means of a piece of hot iron held in a socket within. First recorded about 1760.

ARMILLARY SPHERE   A skeleton celestial globe of metal rings representing the equator, the ecliptic, the tropics, the arctic and antarctic circles, and COLURES.

ARMOIRE   A large cupboard, usually with two doors, generally arranged like a wardrobe with some hanging and some shelf space.

ART NOUVEAU   A rather precious and self-conscious movement in art which, starting in France in the 1890s and 1900s, seemed to offer a way of liberation to spirits numbed by half a century of dreary and bad rehashes of past fashions. Based on soft curves and influenced by the example of Japanese art.

ASH ⟶ **WOODS**

ASTRAGAL   Originally a small moulding of semicircular section placed at the top and bottom of a column, the word is now used to describe the (wooden) mouldings dividing up the glass-fronted door of a piece of furniture (e.g. a bookcase).

ASTROLABE   An early instrument for measuring the (angular) elevation of stars, etc. Its function is now replaced by the use of a sextant.

ATLANTES   Figures or half figures of men used instead of columns to support an **ENTABLATURE** ⟶ **CARYATID**

ATLAS   Paper size ⟶ Table I

AUMBRY = AMBRY

AURICULAR   Shaped like the ear.

AVENTURINE QUARTZ ⟶ **STONES**

AVOIRDUPOIS ⟶ **WEIGHTS** (Table VII)

AZURE ⟶ **HERALDIC TERMS**

B

BAGUETTE-CUT ⟶ **GEM CUTS**

BAIZE ⟶ **TEXTILES**

BALANCE   Of a clock, a bar or wheel which oscillates, allowing the **ESCAPEMENT** to function, and at the same time controlling the speed of movement. One form is the pendulum, whose time of oscillation is governed by its length, not its weight.

BALANCE WHEEL   The **SCAPEWHEEL** of a **VERGE** escapement.

BALLOON CLOCK ⟶ **CLOCKS**

BALTHAZAR ⟶ **BOTTLE SIZES**

BALUSTER   A short round pillar or post, narrow at the top and bulging below; so named for its supposed resemblance to the shape of the wild pomegranate flower.

BANDED AGATE $\longrightarrow$ **STONES**

BANDED JASPER $\longrightarrow$ **STONES**

BANDING   A strip or band of wood of contrasting colour inlaid upon another wood.

BANNER STAND   A piece of furniture, consisting of a banner or other similar framed device, generally embroidered, moveable on a vertical stem set in a firm foot, to protect (the face) from the heat of a fire in a fireplace; also sometimes called a **POLE SCREEN**. In use from the end of the seventeenth century.

BAR $\longrightarrow$ **HERALDIC TERMS**

BARBOLA   Said to be derived from a trade name, it describes a plastic paste used to form coloured models of small objects attached to articles as decoration.

BAROQUE   Irregularly shaped, grotesque, odd, especially of a florid style of late Renaissance architecture or decorating; thus from the early seventeenth century onwards. A **BAROQUE PEARL** is one of irregular shape.

BAROQUE PEARL $\longrightarrow$ **STONES**

BARREL   In watches and clocks the drum housing the mainspring, or, in the case of **LONG-CASE** clocks, that on which the line suspending the weight is wound.

BASAL KICK $\longrightarrow$ **KICK**

BAS-RELIEF $\longrightarrow$ **RELIEF**

BASSE-TAILLE   A technique of enamelling gold whereby the ground is carved out and engraved to receive the transparent **ENAMEL** which is then polished flat with the surrounding gold surface. The design is thus seen as if through a transparent coloured screen.

BASSO RELIEVO/RILIEVO $\longrightarrow$ **RELIEF**

BATON-CUT $\longrightarrow$ **GEM CUTS**

BAT-WING FLUTING   **FLUTING** having a scalloped end.

BAXTER PRINT   Produced by George Baxter (1804–67) this was a form of colour print in which the outline of the picture in one colour was produced from a steel or copper engraving and the remainder of the detail was very accurately imposed by a series, generally 20 to 30 in number, of wood blocks each printing a different colour.

BEAD, BEADING   Small half-round moulding.

Also called **ASTRAGAL**.

BEARING ⟶ **HERALDIC TERMS**

BEELDENKAST   A Dutch word that turns up in auction catalogues; a cupboard or wardrobe having carved (or painted) figures – typically **PUTTI** – on the front.

BEND ⟶ **HERALDIC TERMS**

BEND SINISTER ⟶ **HERALDIC TERMS**

BENDY ⟶ **HERALDIC TERMS**

BERETTINO   A bluish-grey background colour in **MAIOLICA**.

BERGERE   A deep broad arm chair of which both back and arms are upholstered.

BERLIN WOOLWORK   Woollen tapestry made on square-meshed canvas by copying from a design laid out on squared paper. These designs were originally printed in Berlin (from about 1810).

BERYL ⟶ **STONES**

BEZEL   A sloping edge or face.

BIANCO-SOPRA-BIANCO   A technique in **PORCELAIN** decoration consisting of painting with a white pigment on a glaze lightly tinted with blue.

BIGGIN   A kind of coffee pot with a strainer (after the inventor).

BISCUIT ⟶ **CERAMICS**

BLANC-DE-CHINE ⟶ **CERAMIC COLOURS**

BLAZON A shield in heraldry; a coat of arms; a banner bearing the arms; heraldic description of coat of arms.

BLIND-TOOLING ⟶ **TOOLING**

BLOODSTONE ⟶ **STONES**

BLOOM A composition of resin and powdered pumice used for weighting hollow silver candlesticks the lower halves and feet of which were filled with lead after the article had been **HALLMARK**ed.

BLUE-DASH CHARGER Name given to English **TIN-GLAZE** (**DELFTWARE**) dishes (chargers) characterized by blue dashes all round the rim. They date from the seventeenth century.

BOBÈCHE A drip-ring or **DRIP PAN**, often in glass, for a candle-stick.

BOLECTION A moulding which projects in front of the surface of the work decorated as, for example, a raised moulding round a panel.

BOMBÉ, **BOMBE-FRONTED** One of the words that have not quite decided whether they are still French or have shed their accent and become English. Of furniture, bulging or rounded; generally with outward-bulging curves between top and bottom and between the two sides of a surface.

BONBONNIÈRE A dish or box for sweets.

BONE CHINA ⟶ **CERAMICS**

BONHEUR DU JOUR A small eighteenth-century writing-table for a lady's boudoir, charmingly described by one authority as 'suitable for writing nothing more serious than *billets doux*'.

BOOKPLATE A label, usually pasted inside the cover of a book, to indicate ownership. The finer bookplates, being frequently **LITHOGRAPHS**, **ENGRAVINGS**, or other examples of the draughtsman's craft, can be minor works of art themselves.

BOOK SIZES How long is a ball of string? Likewise what is the size of a sheet of paper? There is no single satisfactory answer because in the printing trade there is a plethora of precise answers with esoteric names. The sizes of books, nevertheless, are described by the number of times a single sheet is folded in the course of binding. The commonest resultant progression employs the following terms, generally written in the trade by the numerical symbols indicated, and read with that callous indifference to their Latin origin which was noted in the Introduction.

FOLIO. Folded once, to form 2 leaves (or 4 sides).

4TO (read **QUARTO**). Folded twice, each leaf being one quarter of the original sheet.

8VO (read **OCTAVO**). Folded 3 times.

16MO (read, with supreme disdain, either as **DECIMO SEXTO**, **SEXTO DECIMO**, or even as **SIXTEENMO**). Folded 4 times.

32MO (pretence at Latin breaks down and this is read simply as **THIRTYTWOMO**). Folded 5 times.

Other sizes are used. For example,

18MO (read **OCTODECIMO**, or **EIGHTEENMO**). Such that each leaf is one eighteenth of the original sheet.

For the various sizes of sheets of paper, and the dimensions of books derived from them and employing the sequence defined above, ⟶ Tables II and III. Writing or drawing paper is cut to different sizes from those used for printing, which, for comparison, are included in Table I.

BOTTLE GLASS ⟶ **GLASS**

BOTTLE SIZES The collector of wine, unlike other collectors, is in the strange position that – unless (perish the thought!) he is collecting only as an investment – he must destroy his collection in the company one hopes of a few chosen friends, in order to gain the ultimate satisfaction from it. He need not, however, destroy the containers. Since claret and the red wines of Burgundy mature more slowly and lusciously in large bottles, the very best are sometimes bottled in large sizes. The terminology for these larger bottles is confusing by its inconsistency. The names apply primarily to claret and champagne nomenclature because of the kindred shape of the bottle. Even so it must be remembered that the standard single bottle of claret and burgundy contains 75 centilitres to the 80 centilitres of the standard bottle of champagne. The result is the following:

Capacity	Claret	Champagne
2 bottles	Magnum	Magnum
3 bottles	Marie-Jeanne	Does not exist
4 bottles	Double Magnum	Jeroboam
6 bottles	Jeroboam	Rehoboam
8 bottles	Imperial (*Impériale*)	Methuselah
12 bottles	Does not exist	Salmanazar
16 bottles	Does not exist	Balthazar
20 bottles	Does not exist	Nebuchadnezzar

Burgundy is unlikely to be found in a bottle larger than a Methuselah.

Bottles for red wines from countries other than France, and for the white wines of Alsace, Rhine, and Jura are less consistent in size and in any case do not enjoy biblical or other cognomens.

In conclusion it should be recorded that the soulless Eurocrats seek to introduce a Standard European Bottle holding a miserable 70 centilitres, thus further robbing life of the charm of its infinite variety and subjecting it to Economic Man.

BOULLE A type of decorative inlay on furniture, using pewter, brass, and brown **TORTOISESHELL**, named after the French cabinet-maker Charles André Boulle (1642–1732).

BOURGEOIS $\longrightarrow$ **TYPE SIZES** (Table VI)

BRACKET CLOCK $\longrightarrow$ **CLOCKS**

BRASS $\longrightarrow$ **ALLOY**

BREAKFRONT Of a piece of furniture, like a bookcase, where the central section projects breaking up the flatness of the front surface.

BRECCIA MARBLE $\longrightarrow$ **STONES**

BREVIER $\longrightarrow$ **TYPE SIZES** (Table VI)

BRIEF Paper size$\longrightarrow$ Table I

BRIGHT-CUT   A form of engraving of silver surfaces with deep cuts whose sloping sides are smooth and therefore brightly reflecting.

BRILLIANT-CUT ⟶ **GEM CUTS**

BRIOLETTE-CUT ⟶ **GEM CUTS**

BRITANNIA METAL ⟶ **ALLOY**

BRITANNIA (silver)   A standard of purity for silver ware, meaning a minimum content of 95. 84 per cent (958.4 millesimes) pure silver in the **ALLOY**.

BRITANNIA STANDARD ⟶ **HALLMARKS**

BROCADE ⟶ **TEXTILES**

BRONZE ⟶ **ALLOY**

BRUSHING SLIDE   In a chest of drawers or similar piece of furniture, a single board immediately above the drawers and pulling out like a drawer, on which to place garments for brushing.

BUFFET   (1) A stool or footstool
        (2) A sideboard or side-table for china, **PLATE**, etc.

BULL'S BLOOD ⟶ **CERAMIC COLOURS** (*SANG-DE-BOEUF*)

BULL'S EYE   Small glass window in the door of a **LONG-CASE** clock to enable the pendulum to be seen.

BUREAU   A writing desk with drawers. The writing surface is usually a flap that folds forward resting on runners to take the weight, which when closed forms a top that is triangular in cross section, there being small drawers and pigeon-holes at the back within the writing area. A **FALL-FRONT** bureau, however, is such that the writing flap closes vertically to present a straight-fronted piece of furniture.

BUREAU À CYLINDRE   A **BUREAU** having a solid semi-circular closure, which swivels in to the back when opened.

BUREAU PLAT   A table for writing upon, generally with a single line of drawers immediately beneath the table surface, and often with slides (cf. **BRUSHING SLIDE**) at the two ends, to extend the working surface.

BURNISH   To make smooth and glossy with a hard smooth tool; hence a different process to ordinary polishing.

BURR, BUR   (1) Of woods, having dark circular markings with a lighter ring around.

            (2) The wood of the Banyan tree.

BUTTON PEARL ⟶ **STONES**

C

CABOCHON ⟶ **GEM CUTS**

CABRIOLE   A shape of legs in furniture, like a much elongated 's', and thought to resemble the outline of the hind legs of a horse when performing a cabriole. ⟶ page 47

CACHE-POT   A decorative (usually porcelain) vessel for holding a potted plant and concealing the coarse earthenware pot.

CADDY   A small box with a lid for holding tea – a corruption of the word *kati*, a Malay weight of 1 1/5 lb avoirdupois.

CAIRNGORM ⟶ **STONES**

CALAMANDER ⟶ **WOODS**

CALIBRE ⟶ **GEM CUTS**

CAMEO   A stone such as **ONYX** or **AGATE**, having two layers of different colours, in the upper of which a figure is carved in **RELIEF**, the lower colour serving as background. Also pieces of shell similarly carved. ⟶ **INTAGLIO**

CAMPHOR (WOOD) ⟶ **WOODS**

CANARY DIAMOND ⟶ **STONES**

CANTERBURY   A stand with light partitions to hold music etc.

CAPE ⟶ **STONES (DIAMOND)**

CARAT   (1) Weight for measuring precious stones. ⟶ **WEIGHTS**

            (2) Standard of purity for gold wares. In Britain there are 4 recognized standards, of 22, 18, 14, and 9 carat, which respectively guarantee a minimum content of 91.66, 75.0, 58.5, and 37.5 per cent of pure gold in the object **HALL-MARK**ed. cf. **STERLING**

CARBUNCLE ⟶ **STONES**

CARLTON HOUSE DESK A writing table having drawers and pigeon-holes above the table at the back which curve forward in diminishing tiers on either side to the front. They date from the end of the eighteenth century.

CARNELIAN ⟶ **STONES**

CARNIVAL GLASS Pressed **GLASS** of a smokey orange hue produced for sale at country fairs.

CARRARA MARBLE ⟶ **STONES (MARBLE)**

CARRIAGE CLOCK ⟶ **CLOCKS**

CARTOUCHE Originally a roll of paper, it has become successively an ornament in the form of a scroll, a tablet representing a sheet of paper with the ends rolled up to take an ornament or an inscription, and finally has lost the concept of the roll of paper and has become a space within a decorated edge to take an inscription or design.

CARTRIDGE Paper size ⟶ Table I

CARYATID A female figure used to support an **ENTABLATURE**. ⟶ **ATLANTES**

CASSOLETTE A vessel in which perfume is burned, or a box with a perforated top to diffuse perfume.

CASTER A mis-spelling of **CASTOR**.

CASTOR (1) A small wheel and a swivel attached to the feet of furniture so that the article may be turned without lifting.

(2) A vessel with a perforated top with which to cast pepper, sugar, etc. on food.

CAT'S EYE ⟶ **STONES**

CAUDLE CUP ⟶ **PORRINGER**

CAVETTO A hollow moulding, strictly the quarter of a circle; used for that part of the inside of a dish or plate, between the rim and the base, which is a concave curve.

CELADON A pale leek green colour, principally used to describe a certain Chinese porcelain **GLAZE**. Allegedly named after the green garb of the shepherd Celadon in a play in vogue in France at the time when this porcelain was starting to appear in quantity from China. Equally convincingly it could be derived from a large gift of the porcelain to Salah-ed-Din (Saladin) five centuries earlier during the Crusades. It is produced by covering the vessel with an iron oxide-bearing **SLIP** under the **GLAZE**. In fact the term is applied to quite a range of colours from yellow through pale to dark green. ⟶ **CERAMIC COLOURS**

CELLAR A corruption of the obsolete English *saler*, itself a corruption of the French *salier*, a box of salt. Whence any vessel for holding salt upon the food table. The earliest form was the **STANDING SALT**, which was a large piece, consisting of an open basin or saucer, usually with a cover, on a pillar, which could take any form (e.g. animal, human, architectural) and stood as much as a foot to eighteen inches high.

CELLARET A case or container divided into compartments to hold wine bottles or decanters.

CERAMIC COLOURS AND GLAZES It is suspected that the earliest glazing on ceramic ware was the result of an accident, the falling of wood ash on to the heated clays of vessels within a kiln, and the chemical elements of the ash combining with those in the clay to produce a glaze. Experiment followed to improve and develop this effect, and the addition of different chemical elements was found, as the result of firing, to produce different colours. Further experimentation with different combinations of ingredients and purer forms of the chemicals, together with variations in the firing techniques – primarily in the amount of oxygen admitted – begat a wide variety in the hardness, translucency, and colour of the glazes produced.

When oriental PORCELAIN first reached Europe in any quantity it was the whiteness of the body and the vitreous hardness of the glaze that excited particular admiration, and led to the long experimentation in Europe to discover the secret of making true porcelain.

But it was not only the whiteness of the body that appealed; the shapes, the delicacy of the decoration, and its colours all played their part.

In the earliest importations the monochromes, particularly CELADON and the blue decorations, were the commonest. The blue, in particular, was mostly applied to the BISCUIT before glazing and firing, whence the term UNDERGLAZE (or UNDER-THE-GLAZE) BLUE, though this treatment was not limited to blue. Later came the technique of ENAMEL colouring, distinct from ENAMEL on metal, that is, the application of varied colours upon the already glazed surface (itself often with an UNDERGLAZE design already in place) and their fixing by a further firing at a lower temperature. The use of certain standard groups of colours in which one predominated led to the classifications of *famille rose*, *famille verte*, etc. Meanwhile a number of the monochrome glazes had acquired standard names, which are customarily used of oriental porcelain.

BLANC-DE-CHINE   A clear white; sometimes slightly creamy.

CELADON   A range of bluish or greyish greens varying from deep olive, through lighter tones, to grey. Owing to mistakes in firing the glaze can appear as a muddy yellow or brown.

CLAIR DE LUNE   A very pale powder blue.

IMPERIAL YELLOW A clear bright yellow, sometimes as deep in colour as an egg yolk.

IRON-RED A bright rust colour used in **GLAZES** for porcelain and based upon an oxide of iron. Those who like to blind with science or show off their own erudition will, especially when speaking of French or German ceramics, affectedly prefer to use the terms *ROUGE DE FER* and *EISENROT* respectively for the same thing.

PEACH BLOOM A rich rose pink, sometimes flecked with green.

ROBIN'S EGG BLUE A pale greenish blue flecked with pale buff, like a robin's egg.

SANG-DE-BOEUF (**OX** or **BULL'S BLOOD**) A rich dark red.

TEA DUST A dark brown with flecks of lighter brown.

Among the polychromes the following are the terms most frequently mentioned.

FAMILLE JAUNE **ENAMEL** colours dominated by yellow, often as a ground colour.

FAMILLE NOIRE Similarly, with black as the background colour.

FAMILLE ROSE Similarly, with pinks and crimsons, based on chloride of gold, predominating.

FAMILLE VERTE Similarly, with greens predominating.

Sometimes Chinese terms are used, notably:

SAN TS'AI Three colours.

WU TS'AI Five colours.

In the case of Japan, a place name describes a colouring.

IMARI Red, gold, and green **ENAMELS** on an initial pattern of **UNDERGLAZE BLUE** and white.

CERAMICS This is the most convenient omnibus word (the adjective may be spelt **CERAMIC** or **KERAMIC**) under which to group those that follow, and in the present context means: the art of making what the collector of the most exquisite porcelain will refer to as his 'pots'; or the pottery itself. We can forget, for present purposes, that mixtures of earths with conducting properties are used in modern technology as ceramic electric heating elements, such as the de-mister on the back window of a motor-car; that other mixtures yield the ceramic shield that protects a space capsule and its astronauts from incineration on re-entry to the earth's atmosphere; or that compositions incorporating radio-active metals may form ceramic fuel elements of nuclear reactors. Even in the more limited sphere of art and artefact the various terms overlap.

A *The ingredients*

CHINA-CLAY = KAOLIN

CHINA-STONE = PETUNTSE

CLAY   A stiff viscous earth, consisting mainly of aluminium silicate, and mostly derived from the decomposition of feldspathic rocks: when mixed with water it forms a tenacious paste which may be moulded into any shape and which hardens when dried.

FEL(D)SPAR   Name of a group of minerals, usually white or flesh-red in colour, occurring in crystals or crystalline masses. They consist of silicate of alumina, with soda, potash, lime, etc.

FIRECLAY   A particular mixture of earths, incorporating generally magnesite or dolomite, which has the capacity to withstand very high temperatures; used to make bricks to line fireplaces or kilns.

FRIT   A powdered form of the ingredients of glass used as an alternative to **CHINA-STONE** in making **SOFT-PASTE PORCELAIN**.

GLAZE   The vitreous composition used for glazing pottery; often a thin solution of the same clay as the pot itself, frequently incorporating metallic oxides to give colour after firing.

   ALKALINE GLAZE   Composed of soda or potash and sand, and used on a clay body which contains the same materials. Is tantamount to a form of glass.

COPERTA = *KWAART* = **LEAD GLAZE**

LEAD GLAZE   Composed of oxide of lead, sand, potash, and salt.

SALT GLAZE   Achieved by throwing common salt into the kiln at peak temperature. The soda in the salt volatilizes and combines with the silica and alumina in the clay to form a tight-fitting glass-like glaze of 'orange-peel' texture.

TIN GLAZE   Lead glaze made opaque by the addition of tin oxide. The first European tin-glazed ware was made in Spain and exported through Majorca to Italy. The Italians soon copied the ware, making it particularly at Faenza. The French imported it and called it **FAIENCE**. The Dutch also copied it, making it at Delft, and the English imported it from them, calling it **DELFTWARE**.

KAOLIN (from the Chinese place name, **KAOLIANG**, high hill, whence the substance was first obtained)   A fine white clay produced by the decomposition of **FELDSPAR**, used in the manufacture of porcelain. Today the world's most important deposits are in Cornwall.

PETUNTSE (from the Chinese, meaning white stone)   A white earth consisting of pulverized granite; used in combination with **KAOLIN** in the making of Chinese porcelain.

PIPECLAY   A popular name for the rather impure china clay used for making white clay tobacco pipes; also a verb meaning to apply whitening to fabric.

SLIP   Virtually identical in composition with primitive **GLAZE**: but whereas **GLAZE** is used to produce, after firing, a hard vitreous protective surface, slip is more usually used to decorate and is therefore subject to covering with transparent **GLAZE**.

B   *The products*

BISCUIT   Ceramic ware fired once in the kiln, but not glazed or embellished.

BONE CHINA   See PORCELAIN below.

CHINA   China porcelain, China ware, china. A fine semi-transparent earthenware, brought from China into Europe in the sixteenth century, first by the Portuguese, who named it porcelain (*porcellana*, a word whose etymology is unresolved).

DELFTWARE   Originally Dutch, and subsequently English, tin-glazed EARTHENWARE. See TIN GLAZE above, and FAIENCE and MAIOLICA below.

EARTHENWARE   Vessels made of baked clay such that unless glazed they are porous.

FAIENCE (French, probably from Fayence, the French form of Faenza in Italy, where much ceramic ware was made).   A general term for all porcelain, but especially earthenware with a glaze incorporating oxides of tin. See TIN GLAZE above.

HARD-PASTE   See PORCELAIN below.

MAIOLICA, MAJOLICA   Originally a name for a kind of Italian pottery coated with an opaque white enamel ornamented with metallic colours; later applied to all kinds of glazed Italian ware. See TIN GLAZE above.

PORCELAIN   True porcelain, known also as hard-paste porcelain, originated in China. It is fine, has a translucent body, and a transparent glaze. Its distinguishing feature is that it is made from a mixture of KAOLIN and PETUNTSE. Moistened KAOLIN having high plasticity allows the fashioning of objects of any shape. The PETUNTSE fuses at a temperature of about 1450°C, while the KAOLIN does so at about 1700°C. By firing at the lower temperature complete hardness is achieved without degradation of the clay. The secret of making hard-paste porcelain was only discovered in Europe at Meissen in Saxony, soon after 1700, and was for a time jealously guarded. Attempts, often extremely laborious, to imitate true porcelain with other materials in the absence of KAOLIN produced what is known as soft-paste (or artificial) porcelain. The addition of a percentage of ground calcined animal bone to the raw materials increases the range of firing temperatures and thus reduces the percentage of **WASTERS** in the product. The product is known as **BONE CHINA**.

SOFT-PASTE   See **PORCELAIN** above.

STONEWARE   A hard dense kind of pottery ware made from very siliceous clay, or a mixture of clay with much flint or sand. These substances, when fired to about 1250°C, vitrify so that, unlike unglazed **EARTHENWARE**, stoneware is impervious to liquids.

TERRA-COTTA   A hard unglazed brownish-red pottery of fine quality.

WASTER   Any piece of ceramic ware which has become broken, mis-shapen, or otherwise damaged during the process of firing, and has consequently been discarded. Wasters, which from their nature are generally found in pits or dumps at kiln sites, provide valuable evidence of the nature of the products of old and long-closed kilns, whose surviving perfect products may be very rare.

CHALCEDONY $\longrightarrow$ **STONES**

CHAMFER   (1) A small groove.

(2) The surface produced by bevelling off equally on both sides the corners of a square edge.

CHAMPLEVÉ   Similar to *CLOISONNÉ* except that the compartments are excavated out of the metal base itself, instead of being built up upon it.

CHAPE   The metal plate of a scabbard, particularly that which covers the tip.

CHAPTER RING   The circular band on the dial of a clock containing the figures.

CHARGE $\longrightarrow$ **HERALDIC TERMS**

CHASE   (1) To adorn metal with work embossed or engraved in relief.

(2) To set a gem.

CHASUBLE $\longrightarrow$ **VESTMENT**

CHATELAINE   A belt worn by ladies (originally, by the chatelaine, the mistress of a country house) with short chains attached for carrying keys, scissors, etc.

CHESTERFIELD ⟶ COUCH

CHEVAL-GLASS (also **CHEVAL MIRROR**) A mirror swung on a frame and large enough to reflect the whole figure.

CHEVET ⟶ *TABLE DE CHEVET*

CHEVRON ⟶ HERALDIC TERMS

CHI-CHAO TSUN ⟶ **CHINESE TERMS**

CHIEF ⟶ HERALDIC TERMS

CHIFFONIER (also **CHIFFONNIER, CHIFFONNIERE, CHEFFONNIER**) A small cupboard, with a top forming a side-board.

CHIH ⟶ **CHINESE TERMS**

CH'IH LUNG ⟶ **CHINESE TERMS**

CH'I-LIN ⟶ **CHINESE TERMS**

CH'IN ⟶ **CHINESE TERMS**

CHINA ⟶ CERAMICS

CHINA CLAY ⟶ CERAMICS

CHINA-STONE ⟶ CERAMICS

CHINESE TERMS Any collector of Chinese antiquities requires some acquaintanceship with the Chinese dynasties and the emperors who reigned in each dynasty for the purpose of indicating dating. A list of the dynasties, with their historical dates and the **IDEOGRAPHS** which identify them, is to be found in Table VIII.

In addition there is a host of stock characters or subjects that constantly reappear in decoration, which it would be beyond the scope or purpose of this glossary to enumerate. But an illustration may not be out of place. 'The Three Friends' are pine, bamboo, and plum and their appearance on a gift is a clear expression of the auspicious wish of the giver to the recipient that in his life he shall enjoy the steadfastness of the deep-rooted pine, the flexibility in adversity of the pliant bamboo, and the fragrance of the plum blossom.

Further, there are numerous shapes and decorative motifs or other terms which it has become conventional, because of the inadequacies of translation, to designate by their Chinese names. Some of the more frequently encountered terms, with an indication of their meaning, follow.

Shapes

AN   An oval bowl.

CHI-CHAO TSUN   A water pot, roughly hemispherical, with a flat base and a small aperture at the top.

CHIH   A ritual wine vessel shaped like a beaker vase.

CHIN HU   A pear-shaped wine ewer with a long slender spout and with a long handle on the opposite side.

CHUEH   A ritual wine vessel shaped like an inverted helmet standing on three legs.

FANG LEI   A tall rectangular vase with cover.

FU   A shallow rectangular vessel on feet with a lid of almost identical form.

HSIA   A ritual vessel of cauldron shape with integral tripod legs.

HU   An ovoid vase.

KENDI   A bulbous bottle with a tall neck and a stubby spout.

KU   A ritual wine vessel shaped like a tall flower vase with widely flaring mouth.

KUAN   An ovoid vase, with its broadest part at some two thirds of its height; reminiscent of a Chinese lantern.

KUEI   A bowl-like food vessel.

LIEN TZU   A deep broad bowl on a foot.

MEI P'ING   A tall **BALUSTER**-shaped flower vase with a narrow neck to hold a single bloom.

T'AI PO TSUN   The same as *CHI-CHAO TSUN*.

TING   A tripod cauldron or cooking vessel.

TS'UNG   A square vase with round neck and foot.

YU   A **BALUSTER**-shaped covered pot with handle.

Other Terms

CH'IH LUNG   A form of dragon.

CH'I-LIN   See *KYLIN* below.

CH'IN   A Chinese lute (with five or seven strings).

CH'ING PAI   Blue and white; cf. **YING CHING** below.

FU SHOU AN LING   Four auspicious characters signifying happiness, long life, peace, and spirit.

HEXAGRAM   cf. **TRIGRAM** below.

HONG   A European merchant house or 'factory' in China.

KUAN   Of a glaze, 'official', that is, destined for the imperial household.

KUEI   A mythical beast, a dragon, with only one foot.

KYLIN   A mythical beast, a composite with a deer's body, a bovine tail, horse's hooves, and a horn; a unicorn.

LEI WEN   An archaic decorative motif – 'thunder pattern'.

LING CHIH   A favourite decoration, a magic mushroom, a symbol of long life and prosperity.

NIEN HAO   A reign period; not to be confused with the Emperor's name, a single Emperor having sometimes several reign periods.

PA KUA   The eight **TRIGRAMS**, see below.

PA PAO   The 'Eight Treasures', a set of Buddhist symbols.

SAN TO   Three fruits – peach, pomegranate, and persimmon.

SAN TS'AI   Three colours; thus a style of enamelling porcelain in three colours – usually a dominant background of turquoise or dark green, the other colours being yellow, purple, or dark blue.

SHOU   The Chinese character meaning 'long life'.

T'AO T'IEH   An animal mask, sometimes feline, sometimes bovine, and sometimes composite.

TRIGRAM   The 'eight trigrams' are the eight possible permutations of three lines one below the other, when the lines may be continuous or broken with a space in the middle. They figure in Chinese divination, and each has

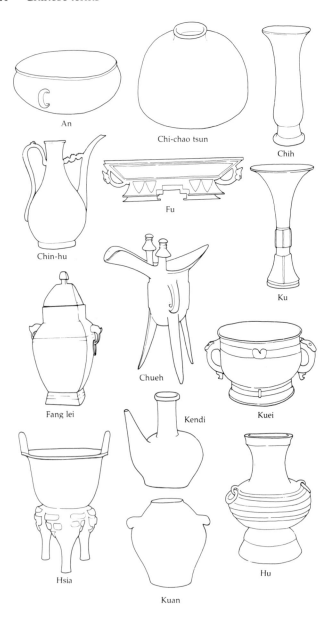

An

Chi-chao tsun

Chih

Chin-hu

Fu

Ku

Fang lei

Chueh

Kendi

Kuei

Hsia

Kuan

Hu

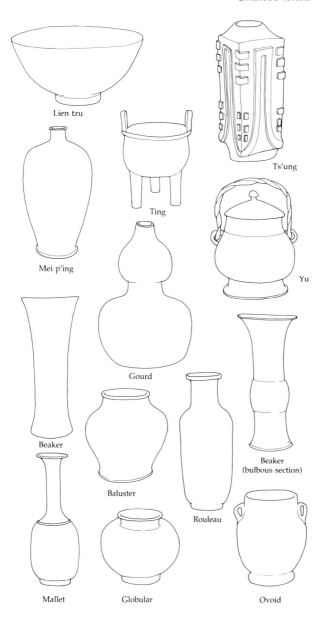

Lien tzu

Ts'ung

Mei p'ing

Ting

Yu

Beaker

Gourd

Baluster

Rouleau

Beaker
(bulbous section)

Mallet

Globular

Ovoid

numerous connotations. When six such lines are set one upon the other (i.e. pairs of trigrams) they are known as hexagrams, and there are naturally sixty-four possible permutations.

WU TS'AI Five colours, whence polychrome (⟶ **SAN TS'AI**), a typical palette being red, yellow, green, turquoise blue, and cobalt blue.

YING CHING A shadowy blue glaze, to which the term *CH'ING PAI* is sometimes erroneously applied.

YUEH-YAO A fabulous beast resembling a winged lion.

CH'ING PAI ⟶ **CHINESE TERMS**

CHIN-HU ⟶ **CHINESE TERMS**

CHINOISERIE Decorations, articles etc., in the Chinese style and, by implication, made in Europe.

CHINTZ ⟶ **TEXTILES**

CHRYSOBERYL ⟶ **STONES**

CHRYSOPRASE ⟶ **STONES**

CHUEH ⟶ **CHINESE TERMS**

CHURCHWARDEN A clay tobacco pipe with a very long stem.

CINNAMON DIAMOND ⟶ **STONES**

CINNAMON STONE ⟶ **STONES**

CIRCULAR CUT ⟶ **GEM CUTS**

CIRE PERDUE A method of casting metal in which the model is covered by a thin uniform coat of wax which is further enclosed in plaster. Molten metal is poured in which, melting the wax, leaves a shell-like casting of the model. The English translation, **LOST WAX**, is also used.

CITRINE ⟶ **STONES**

CLAIR-DE-LUNE ⟶ **CERAMIC COLOURS**

CLAW SET ⟶ **GEM SETTINGS**

CLOCKS The mechanism and dial of a clock can be presented in many forms for various decorative or practical purposes. Some of these have 'standard' names of which some of the commoner are:

BALLOON CLOCK One in which a plain round dial is set on a narrower neck, containing a short pendulum, that broadens out again to a rectangular base serving as a stand.

BRACKET CLOCK Constructed to stand freely on a (matching) bracket affixed to a wall. The typical English bracket clock is in a simple wooden square or rectangular case, with small feet, relying for its elegance on the engraving or other embellishment of the dial, whereas the European continental bracket clock tends to have a much more ornamental case, often with **BAROQUE** or **ROCOCO** embellishment.

CARRIAGE CLOCK Also called a **TRAVELLING CLOCK**, is, as its name implies, a small clock robustly built to withstand the shocks and jolts of carriage travel on bad roads. It is enclosed within a glass-sided bronze or brass frame, and the whole is frequently provided with a padded box with glass front, to provide further protection against damage to its delicate machinery.

LANTERN CLOCK An early type of metal clock reminiscent of a lantern, square in section, and surmounted by the dome-like bell on which the hours are struck.

LONG-CASE CLOCK The formal name for a 'grandfather' or 'grandmother' clock.

MANTEL CLOCK A very broad term for a multiplicity of elegant forms of clock designed to be placed on a mantelpiece, where their function is as much to adorn as to tell the time.

REGULATOR CLOCK A precision **TIMEPIECE** for astronomical work, or for use in a clockmaker's establishment as a standard against which other clocks could be regulated. A compensated pendulum maintains accuracy in changing temperatures, separate dials for hour and minute hands reduce axial friction, and the weight may be set to one side to minimize gravitational influences on the pendulum.

TABLE CLOCK A small clock to stand in the centre of a table, characteristically with a horizontal dial, read from above: but vertical forms are also common.

TRAVELLING CLOCK ⟶ **CARRIAGE CLOCK**

WALL CLOCK Almost any form of clock that is intended to be permanently fixed to a wall – frequently with a large dial, to be readable from a distance, set in a square frame.

CLOISONNÉ (sometimes *CLOISONNÉ* **ENAMEL**) A means of decorating metal with **ENAMEL** in which the various compartments (*cloisons*) of the design are formed by attaching thin metal dividing strips to the metal base: each compartment is then filled with enamel of the requisite colour in the form of powder, and the whole is fired in the furnace. ⟶ *CHAMPLEVÉ*

CLUSTER COLUMN A column made of, or made to look like, several cylindrical columns bound together.

COASTER A low round stand for a decanter.

COCK-BEADING Small **BEAD** projecting beyond an edge, often pinned or glued round drawer fronts.

COFFER (1) A box or chest.
(2) A sunk panel in a ceiling.

COLCOTHAR A brownish red peroxide of iron used as a pigment.

COLD CAST BRONZE Casting made with a viscous composition of fine spherically powdered bronze mixed as a dense paste in a colourless synthetic medium. Parts are joined and the joints ground to give the appearance of a casting in pure metal.

COLLAGE A way of decorating flat surfaces by gluing things to them.

COLLET ⟶ **GEM CUTS**

COLLET SET ⟶ **GEM SETTINGS**

COLLOTYPE ⟶ **PRINT**

COLOMBIER Paper size ⟶ Table I

COLOPHON The inscription or device, originally at the end of a book, giving the title, printer's name, place of printing, and date.

COLURE Each of two great circles which intersect at right angles at the poles on a globe.

COMMODE   A large and elegant piece of furniture of French origin, resembling a chest of drawers. Unlike the latter, which was made for the bedroom, the commode was made for the sitting room, for instance to fill a space between two windows (hence the tendency to be large); sometimes made with drawers, sometimes with cupboard doors, which might conceal shelves or drawers, it was frequently elegantly decorated with **MARQUETRY** or **BOULLE** ornamentation.

COMPAGNIE DES INDES   A term frequently used as a generic name for the Chinese porcelain made expressly for export to Europe and America, and carried by the ships of the various East India Companies. The product was also often known as **EXPORT CHINA**. It has been estimated that in the period from the beginning of the sixteenth to the end of the first third of the nineteenth century some 170–180 million individual pieces of this porcelain were so exported.

COMPORT   A dessert dish raised upon a stem. A word with quite a history! *Compote* (being the French for preserved or stewed fruit) was served in a *compotier*, which word the Englishman took over, inserted an 'r', and then cut off the ending.

COMPOSITE ⟶ **ORDER**

CONSOLE TABLE   A marble-topped surface supported on often ornate brackets, without back legs, designed to be fixed permanently to a wall.

CONTREPARTIE   Technique in **MARQUETRY** whereby when a design has been cut out of one veneer for insertion in another the identically shaped remainders are similarly used to produce a reverse pattern.

CONVERSATION PIECE   A kind of **GENRE** painting of a group of human figures, as though in conversation with each other.

COPE ⟶ **VESTMENT**

COPERTA ⟶ **CERAMICS**

COPY   Paper size ⟶ Table I

CORAL ⟶ **STONES**

CORBEL   A bracket.

CORDOVA LEATHER   Leather work from the Spanish town of Cordova, originally goatskin, and later horse hide, used, apart from shoes, in embossed and coloured panels for decorating walls. The adjectival form, Cordovan, is the origin of the archaic name for a leather-worker, namely cordwainer.

CORINTHIAN ⟶ **ORDER**

CORNELIAN ⟶ **STONES**

COROMANDEL   An erroneous name for **CALAMANDER** wood

CORONET ⟶ page 35

COUCH   It seems that the Anglo-Saxons are much concerned to secure their seated or recumbent comfort. Consider the following collection.

> **COUCH**   Really a bed; but now often used for a piece of furniture, not for the bedroom, on which to recline, having one end raised for the head.
>
> **CHESTERFIELD**   Just as one Earl of Chesterfield gave his name to a type of overcoat, so another gave his to a type of **SOFA**, large, deep, with rather square corners, and very well stuffed, the upholstery, often in leather, being generally 'buttoned', to keep the generous padding in position.
>
> **DAVENPORT**   In America, a type of large **SOFA**.
>
> **DIVAN**   Originally an oriental council of state, the word was extended to that part of a council chamber where the floor was raised and provided with carpets and cushions to provide a place for reclining. Thence, by extension, to the modern bed with neither head nor footboard, which, suitably covered, can be used as a **SOFA** in a living room.
>
> **LOUNGE**   A kind of **SOFA** or easy chair on which one can lie at length.
>
> **SETTEE**   An indoor seat for two or more persons, with a back and, usually, arms, and usually upholstered.
>
> **SETTLE**   A long wooden bench, usually with arms and a high back, and, strictly, having a locker or box under the seat.

EARL
8 pearls on long points
alternating with 8 short
strawberry leaves. In
illustrations, 5 pearls and 4 leaves
are shown.

KING
4 crosses patée alternating with
fleurs-de-lys.
On the king's crown, diadems
spring from the crosses and the
junction is surmounted by a
mount bearing another cross
patée.

VISCOUNT
16 pearls on the rim. In
illustrations only 8 or 9 pearls are
shown.

DUKE
8 strawberry leaves of equal
height; only 5 appearing in
illustrations and when used as a
charge or a crest only 5 showing.

BARON
6 pearls on the rim. In
illustrations only 4 pearls are
shown.

MARQUESS
4 strawberry leaves alternating
with 4 pearls of equal height. In
illustrations, 3 leaves and 2 pearls
are shown.

SOFA Another oriental word, this time Arabic, meaning a raised part of the floor covered with rugs and cushions for sitting. Whence, by evolution, the long stuffed seat with a back and ends (or one end) on which to recline or sit, which the words means to-day.

COVE In architectural use a concave arch or vault; used especially of a concave ceiling, which is then described as **COVED**.

CRACKLE Widely spaced hair cracks in the **GLAZE** of some – particularly Chinese – **PORCELAIN**, deliberately contrived to give an appearance of age.

CRATER ⟶ **KRATER**

CRAZING Fine minute cracks in the **GLAZE** of **PORCELAIN**, the result of a mistake in the glazing.

CREAMER (1) A flat dish for skimming the cream off milk.

(2) In the United States, a cream-jug.

CRENEL(L)ATED Having indentations like a battlement.

CREDENCE TABLE (1) A side table or sideboard on which dishes were placed prior to serving at table. This meaning is now obsolete, but of course is not so in respect of sufficiently old articles.

(2) In the Roman Catholic and Anglican churches, a small table (or shelf) on which to place the elements of the eucharist before their consecration.

CRESTING An ornamental ridge in furniture, architecture etc., resembling a stylized cock's crest or comb.

CREWEL A thin **WORSTED** yarn used for tapestry-style embroidery.

CREWEL-WORK Embroidery in which the design is worked in **CREWEL** on a background of linen or other cloth.

CRISSLED (CRIZZLED) Of **GLASS**, containing a network of fine interior cracks due to excess of alkali in the composition of the material.

CROCKET Small ornament, generally a bud or leaf, on the inclined side of a pinnacle or **FINIAL**.

CROSS-BANDING In cabinet-making, having a veneer laid

upon the surface with the grain of this veneer at right angles to the grain of the wood on which it is laid.

CROSS STITCH ⟶ **STITCHES**

CROWN (1) ⟶ **GEM CUTS**
       (2) Paper size ⟶ Table II

CROWN GLASS ⟶ **GLASS**

CRYSTALLO-CERAMIE A technique, used mostly in glass paperweights, whereby ceramic decoration is introduced into a glass object. The essential feature is that the ceramic should resist a greater heat than that of molten glass. The ceramic is generally a mixture of **CHINA CLAY** and a **FRIT** of potash and sand. The favourite motifs are cameo portraits. Objects of this type are also known as **INCRUSTATIONS** or **SULPHIDES**.

CUIR-BOUILLI Leather boiled or soaked in hot water and then when soft pressed into a shape which it retains when dry and hard.

CULET ⟶ **GEM CUTS**

CULLET Broken glass used in each batch of new glass to promote fusion.

CULTURED PEARL ⟶ **STONES**

CURVETTE A **CAMEO** so cut that the design sits in a hollowed background surrounded by an edge, raised as much as the central design.

CUSHION CUT ⟶ **GEM CUTS**

CUT CARD WORK A term used to describe flat patterns of sheet metal applied to the main body of an object, commonly silver, as decoration.

CYLIX A shallow cup with a tall stem; a *TAZZA*.

CYMA A moulding (of a cornice) consisting of a convex and a concave line; an **OGEE**.

D **DADO** The cubical part of a pedestal between base and cornice; hence the lower part of an interior wall when it is decorated differently from the upper part.

DAMASCENE To ornament metal work – particularly swords – with an inlaid pattern in gold or silver, the craft originally coming from Damascus.

DAMASK ⟶ **TEXTILES**

DATING OF CHINESE ARTICLES Chinese articles, particularly porcelain, were often dated by the inscription on the base of a six character legend. This is read from top to bottom in each column starting from the right. For example:

<table>
<tr><td>曆 (4)</td><td>大 (1)</td></tr>
<tr><td>年 (5)</td><td>明 (2)</td></tr>
<tr><td>製 (6)</td><td>萬 (3)</td></tr>
</table>

would be read	Ta	Ming	Wan	Li	Nien	Chih
	(1)	(2)	(3)	(4)	(5)	(6)

and translated 'Made (in the) year(s of the Emperor) Wan Li
            (6)   (5)   (3) (4)
(in the) Great Ming (Dynasty)'.
    (1)   (2)

Sometimes the two dynastic characters were omitted, the mark consisting then of the last four characters. Sometimes, too, the inscription was written in the more formalized seal style. A list of dynasties and symbols is in Table VIII.

It should be noted however that the presence of a date mark is not a guarantee of a date (or rather, period, since precise years were not specified) of manufacture. Earlier marks were used by later craftsmen (particularly Ming marks in Ch'ing times), not always to perpetrate fraud (for even in those days there were Chinese collectors of Chinese antiques), but often in acknowledgement of the skill of a master being copied, or as an acknowledgement of emulation. The calligraphy itself may betray this, but otherwise an indicated date requires confirmation from a scholarly knowledge of the wares concerned.

DAVENPORT (1) Captain Davenport was a naval captain who required a small writing desk for the confined space in his cabin on a sailing ship. A small desk, then, with sloping top, and drawers opening to the side. The term was in use from about 1790.

(2) In America, however, a Davenport is a large sofa. ⟶ COUCH

DEAL ⟶ WOODS

DECIMO SEXTO ⟶ BOOK SIZES

DECORATIVE PATTERNS ⟶ page 40

DECUS ET TUTAMEN Long ago English 'silver' coins actually contained the metal SILVER to give them intrinsic worth; even longer ago the metal was predominantly SILVER and the dishonest clipped (or filed) the edges to melt down for their own profit, passing on the diminished coin as full worth. To detect these dishonest practices the edges of the coins were milled, or, in the case of the crown piece, embossed with the Latin DECUS ET TUTAMEN, 'an ornament and a safeguard'.

DEGREE CUT ⟶ GEM CUTS

DELFTWARE ⟶ CERAMICS

DEMANTOID GARNET ⟶ STONES

DEMY Paper size ⟶ Tables I and II

DENTIL Each of the small rectangular blocks, which together resemble a row of teeth, set in the moulding of a cornice in the IONIC, CORINTHIAN, and some other ORDERs.

DEVICE ⟶ HERALDIC TERMS

DEXTER ⟶ HERALDIC TERMS

DIAMOND ⟶ STONES

DIAMOND CUT ⟶ GEM CUTS

DECORATIVE PATTERNS

ACANTHUS

ANTHEMIUM

ARABESQUE

BEAD AND REEL

DIAPER

FESTOON

GADROONING

GUILLOCHE

HUSK

KEY PATTERN

LOZENGE

OVOLO

RIBBON

SWAG

VINE

VITRUVIAN SCROLL

DIAMOND-POINT ENGRAVING Engraving done with a stylus of which the tip is set with a fragment of **DIAMOND**.

DIAPER A form of ornament consisting of a pattern of squares, **LOZENGES**, etc.

DIPTYCH An altar-piece or painting on two panels which close like a book. ⟶ **POLYPTYCH, TRIPTYCH**

DISH RING A circular ring, some three inches high and seven or eight inches across, on which to place hot dishes to avoid marking the table. In silver most characteristically a product of Dublin. Also known as **POTATO RING** on the (erroneous) theory that the articles were made to be put on a dish, to hold hot potatoes within the rim.

DISTEMPER A method of painting, usually on plaster, in which the colours are mixed with a glutinous substance soluble in water.

DIVAN ⟶ **COUCH**

DOG TOOTH A pointed moulding resembling a project-ing tooth; characteristic of Norman (Romanesque) architec-ture.

DORIC ⟶ **ORDER**

DOUBLE PICA (TWO-LINE PICA) ⟶ Table VI

DOUBLET A counterfeit gem stone consisting either of two pieces of crystal cemented together with a coloured layer between them, or a thin slice of gem stone cemented on to a piece of glass or inferior stone.

DOWEL A round headless wooden peg or pin used to fasten together two pieces of wood. Can be used of materials other than wood.

DRAW-LEAF Of a table which is extended in length by draw-ing out a leaf or board which is incorporated in the table's construction and stored underneath the end part of its surface.

DRESSER As a sideboard, generally with shelves above, is so called because it was originally a side table in the kitchen on which meat was dressed.

DRIP PAN The saucer-like object at the top of a candlestick for catching melted wax, known also as **GREASE PAN** or *BOBÈCHE*.

DRUGGET A coarse woollen cloth for floor covering; used of felt laid under a carpet.

DRY-EDGE Of **PORCELAIN**, the effect produced by so applying the **GLAZE** that it will not run down to the base and stick to the **SAGGAR** during firing.

DRYPOINT ⟶ **PRINT**

DUMB WAITER An arrangement of revolving round trays set on a central upright, for cruets, dishes, etc. By revolving the trays the services of a waiter were dispensed with.

E

EARTHENWARE ⟶ **CERAMICS**

ÉBÉNISTE The French equivalent of the English cabinet maker, with the distinction, not always precisely observed, that the *ébéniste* did inlaid work while the worker in solid wood was a *menuisier*. The distinction had arisen much earlier when only the most skilled *menuisiers* (carpenters) were entrusted with the use of the then very rare and valuable *EBONY* (*ébène*) for inlay work.

EBONY ⟶ **WOODS**

EGLOMISE ⟶ *VERRE EGLOMISE*

EIGHTEENMO ⟶ **BOOK SIZES**

EISENROT ⟶ **CERAMIC COLOURS** (**IRON-RED**)

ELECTROFORM A technique for making impressions in solid metal, as opposed to wax, from seals (generally **INTAGLIO**) by electrolytic deposition of the metal on the seal.

ELECTRO-PLATE ⟶ **PLATE**

ELECTRUM ⟶ **ALLOY**

ELEPHANT Paper size⟶ Tables I and II

ELM ⟶ **WOODS**

EMERALD ⟶ **STONES**

EMERALD-CUT ⟶ **GEM CUTS**

EMPEROR Paper size⟶ Table I

ENAMEL A semi-opaque form of glass fused on to metal

surfaces to decorate them.⟶ *CLOISONNÉ*, **CERAMIC COLOURS**

ENCAUSTIC   The art or process of encaustic painting, that is, by the process of burning in. Originally it referred to the ancient method of painting with wax colours which were fixed by heat, and thus came to mean a process where heat is used. Hence it is occasionally used for the decoration of porcelain with **ENAMEL** colours.

ENCRUST   To ornament by overlaying with a crust of something precious.

ENGLISH   ⟶ **TYPE SIZES** (Table VI)

ENGRAVING   ⟶ **PRINT**

ENTABLATURE   That part of an **ORDER** which is above the column.

EPERGNE   A centre piece for a dinner table, generally in branched form, each branch holding a small dish, for fruit, sweetmeats, etc. A curious word not existing in French, probably invented by a salesman to appeal to the snobbery of those who found bogus French more *bon ton* than basic English.

E.P.N.S.   ⟶ **PLATE**

ERASED   ⟶ **HERALDIC TERMS**

ESCAPEMENT   The device which allows the last wheel in the **GOING TRAIN** of a clock or watch to move one cog at a time.

ESCRITOIRE   A writing-desk or **BUREAU**.

ESCUTCHEON   (1) Originally a shield-shaped surround or movable cover for a keyhole; hence any metal keyhole plate or inlaid keyhole surround.

                     (2) ⟶ **HERALDIC TERMS**

ETCHING   ⟶ **PRINT**

ETUI (**ETWEE**)   A case for small articles, such as spectacles, needles, etc.

EVERLY 144   ⟶ **GEM CUTS**, under **BRILLIANT**

EVERTED   Turning outwards (used particularly of the rims of vessels).

EXPORT CHINA   ⟶ *COMPAGNIE DES INDES*

F **FACET**   Small cut and polished flat surface of a gem.

FACSIMILE   An exact copy. ⟶ REPLICA

FAIENCE ⟶ CERAMICS

FAIRING   A term for the coarse china figures which used to be sold for small sums at fairs.

FAKE   A 'trick or invention', whence a stylistic imitation, but not a copy. ⟶ REPLICA

FALL-FRONT   Of a desk or similar piece of furniture having a locking front surface in the upper part hinged to fall forward and provide a writing or table surface. ⟶ BUREAU

FAMILLE JAUNE ⟶ CERAMIC COLOURS

FAMILLE NOIRE ⟶ CERAMIC COLOURS

FAMILLE ROSE ⟶ CERAMIC COLOURS

FAMILLE VERTE ⟶ CERAMIC COLOURS

FANCY CUT ⟶ GEM CUTS

FANG LEI ⟶ CHINESE TERMS

FEL(D)SPAR ⟶ CERAMICS

FESTOON   A festival decoration, a chain of leaves, flowers, etc. hanging in a curve between two points.

FIELD   (1) ⟶ HERALDIC TERMS

(2) In prayer rugs the central part with the arch (*MIHRAB*) at the top; in other carpets, the area within the border.

FIGA   A Brazilian word. A representation of the human hand with the thumb thrust through between first and second finger, to ward off the evil eye.

FILAGREE/FILIGREE   Delicate jewellery work made with fine threads or beads of gold or silver.

FINIAL   An ornament, originally on a roof, **PEDIMENT**, or gable, and hence on the top of more or less anything; therefore frequently appears as a knob-like handle for a cover. ⟶ KNOP

FIRECLAY ⟶ CERAMICS

FIRE-DOG ⟶ ANDIRON

FIRE-GILDING ⟶ WATER-GILDING

FIRE OPAL ⟶ STONES

FLAN   A disc of metal before stamping to make a coin; a blank.

FLINT GLASS   ⟶ **GLASS**

FLINT-LOCK   A **GUN-LOCK** in which a flint in the cock, striking the metal of the hammer, produces sparks which ignite the priming.

FLOCK   A lock of wool, a tuft of wool or cotton; hence such material used for stuffing upholstery.

FLOCK WALLPAPER   A paper intended to produce cheaply a substitute for silk **BROCADE** or **VELVET** as a wall covering; made by scattering sheared wool on a design outlined on paper in a slow-drying adhesive, giving a cut-velvet effect.

FLUTED   Decorated with **FLUTING**.

FLUTING   Decoration consisting of semi-circular channels, each called a flute, because of supposed resemblance to a half of the musical instrument of the same name, split lengthwise, laid side by side. ⟶ **GADROONING**

FOB   A fob is really a pocket in the trouser waistband for carrying a watch or money; but the word is now used for a fob-chain attached to a watch so carried, and hence to the bar for placing through a button-hole which is attached transversely to the fob-chain.

FOILING   Of a precious stone, having a layer of bright metal foil placed at the back, to act as a reflector and impart greater brilliance.

FOOLSCAP   Paper size⟶ Tables I and II .

FOLIO   ⟶ **BOOK SIZES**

FORGERY   Something made in fraudulent imitation of another, whence a copy designed to deceive. ⟶ **REPLICA**

FOU SHU AN LING   ⟶ **CHINESE TERMS**

FRENCH POLISH   A hard glossy polish on woodwork achieved by applying successive coats of shellac dissolved in alcohol, and rubbing down with fine glass-paper after each successive coat has been applied. Requiring much work and patience, French polishing is little carried out today. Easily applied chemical compounds are used in an unsuccessful attempt to produce as hard, clear, and glossy a finish.

FRESCO A form of painting in water-colour on plaster or mortar which is not quite dry.

FRESHWATER PEARL ⟶ **STONES**

FRET ⟶ **KEY PATTERN**

FRETWORK Wood or metal cut in a pattern, either free-standing, or applied to a surface as ornament.

FRIEZE A band of painted or sculptured decoration.

FRIT ⟶ **CERAMICS**

FU ⟶ **CHINESE TERMS**

FURNITURE: FEET AND LEGS ⟶ page 47

FUSEE A piece of metal shaped like a truncated cone, with a flange at the base, round which a spiral groove is cut to take a gut or chain. Its purpose is in watches and clocks to equalize the drive on the **BARREL** of the mainspring as the latter unwinds.

G

GADROONING Decoration, usually of an edge, consisting of a succession of half-round ridges, often curvilinear, laid side by side. ⟶ **FLUTING**

GALLIPOT A small glazed earthenware pot, especially one used by apothecaries for ointments.

GARDANT, GUARDANT ⟶ **HERALDIC TERMS**

GARNET ⟶ **STONES**

GARNITURE DE CHEMINÉE Set of porcelain ornaments to decorate a mantel-piece. Characteristically three, five, or seven pieces, they are generally vases and beakers, but could include a central clock or a pair of matching candlesticks.

GAUFFER ⟶ **GOFFER**

GEM CUTS Gems may be cut and polished in an infinite variety of ways. Within the limitation imposed by the shape of the rough stone, and sometimes also by its crystalline structure, experience has proved that certain shapes or certain combinations of **FACETS** are the most appropriate

FURNITURE: FEET AND LEGS

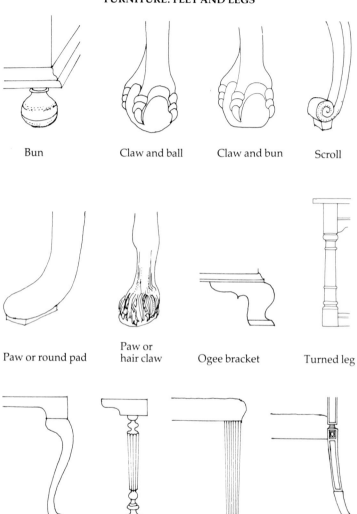

Bun

Claw and ball

Claw and bun

Scroll

Paw or round pad

Paw or
hair claw

Ogee bracket

Turned leg

Cabriole
(18th century)

Turned tapered
(c. 1690)

Square tapered
(c. 1775)

Sabre
(c. 1815)

either to bring out the colour and lustre of a given stone or to create a desired effect when it is set in a piece of jewellery. These standard ways of cutting have each their own name.

The circumference of a stone at its broadest place is called the **GIRDLE**: that part which lies above the girdle is called the **CROWN**; if the crown terminates in a flat surface parallel to the plane of the girdle, it is called the **TABLE**; the part of the stone lying below the girdle is called the **PAVILION**: if the pavilion terminates in a flat surface, parallel to the table, this surface is called the **CULET**, or **COLLET**.

BAGUETTE CUT   Of a long narrow rectangular stone, having a large rectangular table and a single sloping facet on each side to the girdle.

BATON CUT = BAGUETTE CUT

BRILLIANT CUT   The most effective cut for the diamond, the proportions and the angles of the facets having been mathematically calculated to maximize the reflection and refraction of the light entering the stone and thus to create maximum brilliance. The girdle is circular. The brilliant cut has 33 facets above the girdle and 25 below.

The crown should be approximately one-third of the total depth of the stone, this depth being approximately three-fifths of the diameter of girdle. The diameter of the table is approximately half that of the girdle. Both triangular and four-sided facets are used in this cut.

American lapidaries have devised a development of the brilliant cut, which they claim has an average 32 per cent greater brilliance. They have patented it under the name of **EVERLY 144**. It has 33 facets on the crown, 38 around the girdle, and 73 on the pavilion.

BRIOLETTE CUT   An egg-shaped, oval, or pear-shaped stone having its entire surface cut in triangular facets, like a **ROSE CUT**.

CABOCHON CUT   Strictly, a shape rather than a cut, since it is not faceted. Having a domed top of high or low curvature, and a base which may be anything from a repetition of the top to one which is hollowed out, but which is most frequently flat. The girdle can be round or oval.

CALIBRE CUT   Similar to **BAGUETTE CUT**, but a squarer rectangle; cut to fit a specified space.

CIRCULAR CUT   Having a girdle that is a perfect circle: a round **BRILLIANT CUT**.

CUSHION CUT   A rounded **BRILLIANT CUT**.

DEGREE CUT = **STEP CUT**

DIAMOND CUT   Used of stones other than diamonds to indicate that they are cut with facets like a diamond.

EMERALD CUT = **STEP CUT**

FANCY CUT   Modification of the **TRAP CUT** with fancy geometrical outline.

KITE CUT   Describes the four-sided outline of a child's kite, the cutting being based on **STEP CUT** fashioning.

LOZENGE CUT   Shaped in outline like the diamond of a pack of cards, the fashioning based on the **STEP CUT**.

MARQUISE CUT   **BRILLIANT CUT** applied to a pointed oval stone.

OBUS CUT   **EMERALD CUT** applied to a five-sided stone having one square end and one pointed end, so that the outline resembles a bullet or shell.

PENDELOQUE CUT   **BRILLIANT CUT** applied to a pear-shaped stone.

ROSE CUT   A hemispherical stone, having a flat base and a geodesic dome, that is, a dome composed of triangular facets, either 12 or 24, terminating in a point. Used for small stones.

SEAL CUT   Similar to **STEP CUT** but having a very shallow crown and a wide table.

STEP CUT   For square or oblong stones, having a series of rectangular facets parallel to the girdle; the corners may be modified. The pavilion terminates in a point.

TABLE CUT = **STEP CUT**: a truncated pyramid or octahedron.

TRAP CUT = **STEP CUT**.

ZIRCON CUT   Similar to the brilliant cut but having an extra set of facets on the pavilion extending from the culet half-way up the back facets.

GEM SETTINGS   There are various ways in which a gemstone can be held in the metal in combination with which a jewel is fashioned. Each method has its name and the stone is then described as so set.

    CLAW SET   Held by a number of small claws of the metal which are turned over the front edge of the stone.

    COLLET SET   Held in a ring of the metal whose upper edge is then turned over to provide a flange covering the whole circumference of the stone.

    GIPSY SET, **GYPSY SET**   Held by being let into holes in a flat surface of the metal.

    INVISIBLY SET   When the means of fastening cannot be seen from the front of the gem.

    MIRAGE SET   An elaboration of **CLAW** setting when under the claws and above the stone and extending beyond its girdle a ring of metal, itself faceted, is inserted, to give an illusion of a larger stone, and additional sparkle from the facets of the metal.

    PAVÉ **SET**   Applying only to several stones set close together like the stones of a pavement so that no metal is seen between the stones.

GENRE PAINTING   Painting portraying scenes from ordinary life.

GEODE   A rounded stone having a cavity lined with crystals, particularly of the **QUARTZ** family, or other mineral matter.

GERMAN SILVER ⟶ **ALLOY**

GESSO   A substance made of whiting, linseed oil, and size, much used in Europe, especially in the eighteenth century; applied thinly as a basis for gilding and colouring, especially to picture and mirror frames.

GHIORDES KNOT   Knot, originally of Turkish origin, used in handmade oriental carpets.

GILD   To cover with a thin layer of gold; whence, by extension, to cover with a golden colour (e.g. **GILTWOOD**). Both

GILT and **GILDED** are correct forms for the past participle.

GILT $\longrightarrow$ **GILD**

GILT-TOOLING $\longrightarrow$ **TOOLING**

GILTWOOD $\longrightarrow$ **GILD**

GIPSY-SET $\longrightarrow$ **GEM SETTINGS**

GIRANDOLE   (1) A branched support for candles.

(2) An ear-ring or pendant, especially one with a central stone surrounded by smaller stones.

GIRDLE $\longrightarrow$ **GEM CUTS**

GLASS   The basic substance is made by fusing together sand (silica) and soda or potash (or both), with the addition of various other substances such as lime, alumina, or lead oxide to produce various qualities. This gives rise to a number of standard terms noted below.

In nature some combinations of these substances are sometimes fused together in volcanic circumstances and this natural glass, resembling black bottle glass, is **OBSIDIAN**.

BOTTLE GLASS   This means no more than the ordinary coarse type of glass of which bottles are made.

CROWN GLASS   Glass composed of silica, potash, and lime (without metallic elements) and made into circular sheets by blowing and whirling.

FLINT GLASS   A particularly lustrous kind of glass made from sand, alkali, and lead oxide; originally the sand in this composition was ground flint. Flint is the greyish matter within the white cover which together form a flint-stone pebble or nodule, and is one of the purest forms of silica.

LEAD GLASS   A glass made with the addition of a large quantity of lead, of high refractive index, and thus particularly suited for cutting and faceting. Lead glass is often the base of artificial gems.

SODA GLASS   Soda (like potash) being an alkali, soda glass is a term to indicate that this particular alkali is the one that has been used in manufacture.

GLASTONBURY CHAIR   A type of folding chair consisting of two rows of S-shaped members folding along an axis under the leather seat. Supposed to have derived from a sixteenth-century folding chair owned by the last Abbot of Glastonbury.

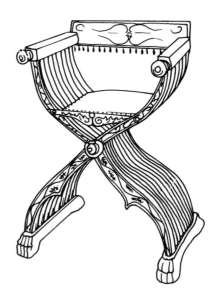

GLAZE ⟶ **CERAMICS COLOURS AND GLAZES**

GLYPH A sculptured mark or symbol; in architecture, a groove or channel.

GOBLET A glass with a stem and foot, as distinct from a **TUMBLER**.

GOFFER (GAUFFER) To make wavy by means of a heated goffering-iron; to crimp (e.g. lace and frills). Of bookbinding and printing, to emboss or imprint with ornamental figures.

GOING TRAIN ⟶ **TRAIN**

GOLD ⟶ **ALLOY**

GOLD-TOOLING ⟶ **TOOLING**

GORGONEION A representation of a Gorgon's head.

GOSHENITE ⟶ **STONES**

GOUACHE A method of painting with opaque colours ground in water and mixed with honey and gum. Whence, a painting so painted, and also the pigment itself.

GRACE-CUP A cup of liquor passed round after grace is said at meals; also the last cup drunk before retiring or parting. Hence sometimes used for **LOVING-CUP**.

GRAFFITI ⟶ **GRAFFITO**

GRAFFITO (pl. **GRAFFITI**) A drawing or writing scratched on a wall or other surface. Whence a method of decoration by scratching through a thin layer of plaster, glaze, etc. on a ground of a different colour. Graffiti, in the sense of scribblings on walls, tend to be rude, and their collection is somewhat eclectic.

GRAM ⟶ **WEIGHTS**

GRAND EAGLE Paper size ⟶ Table I

GREASE PAN ⟶ **DRIP PAN**

GREAT PRIMER ⟶ **TYPE SIZES** (Table VI)

GREEK WAVE-PATTERN ⟶ **VITRUVIAN SCROLL**

GRIFFIN ⟶ **HERALDIC TERMS**

GRISAILLE A form of decorative painting in grey monotone to represent objects in relief.

GROGRAM ⟶ **TEXTILES**

GROSGRAIN ⟶ **TEXTILES**

GROS POINT ⟶ **STITCHES**

GROSSULAR GARNET ⟶ **STONES**

GROTESQUE Decoration in which portions of human and animal forms are fantastically interwoven with foliage and flowers; comically distorted figures, particularly human masks, and designs.

GRYPHON ⟶ **HERALDIC TERMS**

GUÉRIDON A French piece of furniture, a small rectangular table, with two or three shallow drawers, and often a stone top, characteristically placed on either side of a fire-place.

GUGLET A small bottle.

GUILLOCHE A form of ornament or decoration consisting of two or more bands or strings twisting over each other in spiral form. It can be moulding or simply a pattern.

GULES ⟶ **HERALDIC TERMS**

GULLI HENNA One of the classical patterns on Persian carpets, a formalized rendering of the flower of the henna plant; usually a straight stem with stylized daisy-like flowers on each side.

GUN-LOCK That part of the mechanism of a gun by which the charge of powder is ignited.

H

HALF-TONE BLOCK ⟶ **PRINT**

HALLMARK Mark imparted by punches to articles of precious metal to guarantee, after scrupulous test or assay, a statutory degree of purity. In Britain Halls of Assay have been marking silver and gold plate for upwards of six and a half centuries, standards having been prescribed by Henry III in 1238 and hallmarking having been instituted by a Statute of Edward I in 1300.

Essentially the mark consists of four stamps or punches, the maker's mark, the quality mark, the mark of the Hall of Assay, and the year mark. A fifth mark, the sovereign's head in profile, has been added at certain periods of history: from 1784 to 1890, to denote payment of duty; in 1935, together with the consort's head, to mark the silver jubilee of King George V and Queen Mary; in 1953 to mark the accession of Queen Elizabeth II; and in 1977 to mark her silver jubilee.

The maker's mark, in early days often an emblem, is now the initials of the maker or firm submitting the article for assay.

The quality mark is for England a lion **PASSANT**, for Scotland a thistle, for Glasgow was a lion **RAMPANT**, and the **BRITANNIA** quality mark is a seated figure of Britannia. The

GOLD quality mark is a figure showing the CARAT standard, while that for PLATINUM is an orb and cross.

There are at present four Halls of Assay, now called Assay Offices, in the United Kingdom, namely London, Sheffield, Birmingham, and Edinburgh, each with its distinctive mark. In the past there were provincial Assay Offices at Exeter, Newcastle, Norwich, York, Glasgow, and Chester. All have, or had, their distinctive town mark.

The year mark is complicated. Each Assay Office uses a different alphabetic series, but not all 26 letters of the alphabet, changing the style of lettering and the shield in which it lies at the end of the series. London changes its letter within a given cycle in May, Birmingham and Sheffield in July, and Edinburgh in October. Published lists of letters must therefore be consulted for accurate dating.

Other countries have different systems for marking their precious metals, not all under such stringent statutory control. Articles imported into Britain for sale must be submitted for assay, and certain different punches are used.

In order to eliminate some of the problems described in the last paragraph the countries of the European Free Trade Association in 1972 signed a convention agreeing on certain common control marks to be placed on articles of gold, silver, and platinum entering into international trade, which would exempt such articles from further domestic hallmarking on entry into the countries which ratify the convention. Under this convention the common standards of fineness accepted by weight of fine metal in 1000 parts of alloy are:

(1) For gold, 750, 585, and 375.
(2) For silver, 925, 830, and 800.
(3) For platinum, 950.

These correspond: (1) for gold, to 18, 14, 9 carat; (2) for silver, to sterling and two qualities not recognized for assay in Britain. For platinum there has been no prescribed standard in Britain, but by the Hallmarking Act 1973 the standard described above, together with a new mark, an orb and cross, become statutory requirements from 1 January 1975.

⟶ **PLATE, PLATINUM**   Table IX.

HAMMOCK CHAIR   One in which the seat and back are provided by a piece of fabric or leather attached to two horizontal bars, one low in front and the other high at the back.

HAND CHAIR   An alternative name for an upright chair.

HARD PASTE ⟶ **CERAMICS**

HARDSTONE ⟶ **STONES**

HAREWOOD ⟶ **WOODS**

HATCHMENT   An **ESCUTCHEON**, especially a square or lozenge-shaped tablet, showing the armorial bearings of a deceased person.

HELIODORE ⟶ **STONES**

HERALDIC TERMS   Heraldic emblems often decorate works of art. They are described with their own unique vocabulary, deriving from medieval French and Middle English. It is perhaps easiest, without pretensions to accuracy, to think of heraldry, an attribute of the nobility and gentry, as originating at a time when there were no surnames, everyone was called John, and war took precedence over law. A simple emblem on the plain surface (**FIELD**) of the shield helped to distinguish friend from foe. Victories could be recorded, and recalled to the adversary, by additional emblems, each added emblem being a new **CHARGE** or **BEARING**. As the arts of peace succeeded those of war the distinguishing marks survived, with added embellishment to make manifest succeeding relationships and aggrandizements. Strange beasts were called in aid to support the overcharged shield, and battle cries or family mottoes were inscribed above, beneath, or around. The foregoing somewhat imaginative portrayal is reflected in part by the following selection from the catalogue of exotic terms employed.

ARGENT   Silver, therefore white.

AZURE   Blue.

BAR An honourable **ORDINARY**, formed like the **FESSE**, but narrower and covering one-fifth or less of the **FIELD**.

BEARING A single **CHARGE** or **DEVICE**.

BEND An **ORDINARY** drawn from the **DEXTER CHIEF** to the **SINISTER** base, containing one-fifth, or, if charged, one-third, part of the **FIELD** in breadth – i.e., a diagonal stripe from top right to bottom left.

BEND-SINISTER As **BEND**, but from top left to bottom right; an emblem of bastardy.

BENDY Having the field divided into an even number of **BENDS**.

CHARGE = **BEARING**. Marking, design, or emblem placed upon a plain shield.

CHEVRON A broad arrow without the shaft – i.e. a lance-corporal's stripe.

CHIEF The upper third of the **FIELD**.

DEVICE An emblematic figure or design, especially one borne by a particular person, as a heraldic **BEARING**.

DEXTER Right-hand side, right.

ERASED Of the head or other part of an animal, having a jagged edge, as if torn off – e.g. the Leopard's head used as the London **HALLMARK** on **BRITANNIA** standard silver.

ESCUTCHEON The shield on which a coat of arms is depicted.

FESSE Horizontal stripe across the middle of a shield.

FIELD The surface of a shield.

GARDANT, GUARDANT Having the full face towards the spectator.

GRYPHON (GRIFFIN) A fabulous creature (and therefore apt to appear in heraldic representation) having the head and wings of an eagle and the body and hindquarters of a lion.

GULES Red.

IMPALE To bring together two coats of arms side by side on one shield divided by a **PALE**.

OR Gold, therefore yellow.

ORDINARY A **CHARGE** of the simplest kind.

PALE A vertical stripe in the centre of a shield, occupying one-third of its width.

PARTI-BENDY Divided into two different colours by a **BEND**.

PASSANT Of a beast, walking towards the left side and looking towards the left side, with the right fore-paw raised.

QUARTER   To divide a shield into quarters or any number of divisions by vertical and horizontal lines.

RAMPANT   Standing on the left back leg, with both forelegs raised, the right above the left, and with the head in profile.

REGARDANT   Looking backwards.

SABLE   Black.

SALTIRE   A cross formed by a **BEND** and a **BEND-SINISTER** – i.e. a St Andrew's Cross.

SEJANT   Sitting, especially of an animal, with forelegs up-right.

SINISTER Left-hand side, left.

STATANT Of an animal, especially a lion, standing in profile with all four feet on the ground.

SUPPORTER Animal or person supporting one side of the shield in a coat of arms.

TINCTURE Colour.

VERT Green.

WYVERN An imaginary creature represented as a winged dragon with two feet like those of an eagle and a snake-like barbed tail

HERATI An all-over repetitive pattern on many Persian carpets, built up from variations on the theme of a rosette surrounded by leaves.

HESSONITE GARNET $\longrightarrow$ **STONES**

HEXAGRAM $\longrightarrow$ **CHINESE TERMS**

HIGHBOY $\longrightarrow$ **TALLBOY**

HIGH RELIEF $\longrightarrow$ **RELIEF**

HOLLY $\longrightarrow$ **WOODS**

HOLOGRAPH A **MANUSCRIPT** in the handwriting of its author.

HONG $\longrightarrow$ **CHINESE TERMS**

HORNBOOK A small wooden bat, shaped like a battledore, on which was fixed a paper inscribed or printed with the alphabet, the whole covered with translucent horn. Going back to the sixteenth century, it was used to teach children their letters. The handle was usually perforated so that a string could be placed through and the whole hung around the child's neck.

HSIA $\longrightarrow$ **CHINESE TERMS**

HU $\longrightarrow$ **CHINESE TERMS**

HUSK As a decorative motif, resembling the outer shell of a beech-nut. $\longrightarrow$ page 40

ICON An image, representation, or portrait, whence, in its **I** most common use, in the Eastern Church, a representation of a sacred personage (often in an elaborate frame), itself honoured as sacred, and accorded relative worship.

ICONOGRAPH A drawing or illustration for a book.

ICONOSTASIS In the Eastern Church the screen between the sanctuary and the main body of the church, on which the **ICON**s are placed.

IDEOGRAM (IDEOGRAPH) A written symbol conveying the idea of a thing without naming it, as in the Chinese and Japanese written scripts, and capable of being pronounced in various ways according to context. Thus in English the arithmetic sign '+' is an ideogram that may be read 'plus', 'more', or 'added to', according to context. ⟶ **PICTOGRAM**

IKON ⟶ **ICON**

ILLUMINATION The decoration, particularly of an initial letter, of a **MANUSCRIPT**, with gold, silver, and brightly coloured designs or pictures.

IMARI ⟶ **CERAMIC COLOURS**

IMBRICATE So to arrange as to overlap, like roof tiles.

IMPALE ⟶ **HERALDIC TERMS**

IMPASTO Of a style of painting, the laying on of colour thickly, like a paste.

IMPERIAL (1) ⟶ **BOTTLE SIZES**
             (2) Paper size ⟶ Table II

IMPERIAL YELLOW ⟶ **CERAMIC COLOURS**

INCRUSTATIONS ⟶ *CRYSTALLO-CERAMIE*

INCUNABULA The singular form of this word, incunabulum, is seldom encountered; in the commoner plural it is used of early printed books, especially those printed before 1500.

INCUSE Hammered or stamped in; for example of a figure stamped into a coin in **INTAGLIO**.

INRO Japanese personal medicine box, consisting of three or four shallow trays slotted tightly into each other, and held together with a cord, tightening by being passed through a bead, or *OJIME*, the whole being suspended from the belt by a *NETSUKE*. *INRO* are frequently very beautifully decorated with lacquer or carving.

INTAGLIO A design incised or engraved, especially in a stone or other hard material. Whence anything, particularly a gem, so ornamented. Reverse of **RELIEF**. ⟶ **CAMEO**

INCRUSTATION ⟶ *CRYSTALLO-CERAMIE*

INVISIBLY SET ⟶ **GEM SETTINGS**

IONIC ⟶ **ORDER**

IRON-RED ⟶ **CERAMIC COLOURS**

IRON-SPOT A form of **CERAMIC** decoration consisting of iron-brown blobs on a white ground.

IVORY Comes mostly from the tusk of the elephant, the best being the African elephant; but it also comes from the tusk of the mammoth, narwhal, walrus, and boar, and the tooth of the hippopotamus. It is naturally yellow on the surface and white within, but inner layers exposed by carving turn yellow with age.

J

JACINTH ⟶ **STONES**

JADE ⟶ **STONES**

JADEITE ⟶ **STONES**

JAMB Each of the vertical side posts of a doorway, window, or chimney-piece.

JARDINIÈRE An ornamental stand or receptacle for plants, flowers, etc.

JARGOON ⟶ **STONES**

JASPER ⟶ **STONES**

JEROBOAM ⟶ **BOTTLE SIZES**

JET ⟶ **STONES**

JOURNEYMAN CLOCK A secondary clock in an observatory, used to compare with standard clocks.

KAOLIN ⟶ **CERAMICS**

KENDI ⟶ **CHINESE TERMS**

KERAMIC ⟶ **CERAMICS**

KEYFRET ⟶ **KEY PATTERN**

KEY PATTERN, KEYFRET, FRET   A repetitive pattern, derived from classical Greek architecture, made up of straight lines intersecting at right angles. ⟶ page 40

KICK, KICK-UP, BASAL KICK, PUSH-UP   That part of the base of a bottle which is raised within the bottle.

KINGWOOD ⟶ **WOODS**

KITE-CUT ⟶ **GEM CUTS**

KNOP   A small rounded protuberance, whence a knob, stud, button, tassel, etc. ⟶ **FINIAL**

KRATER, CRATER   From Greek antiquity, a large vessel of vase shape with two handles, in which wine was mixed with water.

KRAUTSTRUNK   A glass reliquary.

KU ⟶ **CHINESE TERMS**

KUAN ⟶ **CHINESE TERMS**

KUEI ⟶ **CHINESE TERMS**

KWAART ⟶ **CERAMICS**

KYLIN ⟶ **CHINESE TERMS**

KYLIX = CYLIX

K

LAC   The dark red exudation produced on certain trees when punctured by the insect *coccus lacca*. ⟶ **SHELLAC**

LACQUER   (1) Any of various kinds of resinous varnish, especially that produced in Japan, China, and India, capable of taking a hard polish, applied in numerous successive coats, each polished before the application of the next and often decorated by the admixture of gold dust or colours.

(2) A varnish, chiefly made from shellac dissolved in alcohol, and lightly tinted, for application to metal, especially brass, as a protection against oxidation.

L

LAMBREQUIN   Originally a scarf or piece of stuff worn over a helmet as a covering, and drawn in **HERALDIC** representations with one end, cut or jagged, as floating, it has come to mean:

(1) a short curtain, with the lower edge straight or scalloped, over a door or window or beneath the edge of a mantelpiece;

(2) in the decoration of ceramics a band of solid colour with its lower edge jagged or scalloped.

LANTERN CLOCK   ⟶ **CLOCKS**

LAPIS LAZULI   ⟶ **STONES**

LAPPET   An overlapping part of a garment or decoration. A hanging part.

LATTEN   ⟶ **ALLOY**

LATTICE-WORK   A structure of wooden laths or metal strips with spaces between to form a screen: sometimes applied to a flat surface as decoration.

LATTICINIO   Lace-glass; clear glass with embedded rods of opaque white glass forming a pattern.

LAZY SUSAN   A circular cheese dish with a swivelling cover, so that the dish may be closed without the effort of lifting a lid.

LEAD GLASS   ⟶ **GLASS**

LEAD GLAZE   ⟶ **CERAMICS**

LEI WEN   ⟶ **CHINESE TERMS**

LIEN TZU   ⟶ **CHINESE TERMS**

LIGNUM VITAE   ⟶ **WOODS**

LIME   ⟶ **WOODS**

LING CHIH   ⟶ **CHINESE TERMS**

LINDEN   ⟶ **WOODS**

LINENFOLD   A carved ornament for a panel, representing a fold of linen.

LINO-CUT   ⟶ **PRINT**

LITHOGRAPH   ⟶ **PRINT**

LITHOPHANE   A panel of highly glazed **HARD-PASTE** porcelain which when illuminated from the front appears to be very crude **INTAGLIO**, but which when illuminated from behind has tones and definition as subtle and delicate as a photograph. The manufacturing process was first patented in 1827, thus antedating photography. The majority were made in Germany.

LITHOTINT ⟶ **PRINT**

LONG-CASE CLOCK ⟶ **CLOCKS**

LONGCHAIN Apt to appear as a single word in auctioneers' catalogues of jewellery, it means no more than a long chain.

LONG RUNNER ⟶ **TYPE SIZES**

LOO TABLE Large, generally round or octagonal, table on a central pillar; the name comes from the card game, loo, or lanter-loo, played on such tables.

LOST WAX ⟶ *CIRE PERDUE*

LOUNGE ⟶ **COUCH**

LOVING-CUP A large drinking vessel, usually of silver, and frequently ornate, passed from hand to hand at the end of a banquet, often with considerable ceremony, so that each guest may drink in turn and testify to friendship with his neighbours. ⟶ **GRACE-CUP**

LOWBOY A single chest of drawers, standing on legs, from which often detachable. The term is more of American than British usage. ⟶ **TALLBOY**

LOW RELIEF ⟶ **RELIEF**

LOZENGE In decoration, four-sided equilateral figure with two acute and two obtuse angles; the shape of the diamond in a pack of cards.

LOZENGE CUT ⟶ **GEM CUTS**

LUNETTE A fan or half-moon shaped decorative *motif*, the area within the borders frequently carved.

LUNETTE-CUT ⟶ **GEM CUTS**

LUSTRE WARE Pottery with a glaze in bright and shiny metallic colours. Most commonly the colours are gold or orange, and silver, but pink, mottled pink, and dark copper colours are made.

LUTING The use of liquid clay or slip to assemble various parts of ceramic ware or to apply decoration to the surface of such ware.

M   *MACRAMÉ*   A special form of knotting, used to make fringes or trimmings.

MAGNUM ⟶ **BOTTLE SIZES**

MAHOGANY ⟶ **WOODS**

MAIOLICA/MAJOLICA ⟶ **CERAMIC**

MALACHITE ⟶ **STONES**

MANTEL CLOCK ⟶ **CLOCKS**

MANTLING   In **HERALDIC** design an ornamental accessory of drapery or scroll-work depicted behind and around an escutcheon granted in recognition of an achievement. ⟶ **LAMBREQUIN**

MANUSCRIPT   Before printing was invented all writing had to be by hand, and a manuscript was a hand-written work. But the centuries that intervened between the invention of the printing press and the typewriter brought a subtle change, so that the manuscript became a 'not printed' work. Accordingly, after the invention of the typewriter, a manuscript (particularly that of an author) was able happily to include a typescript. ⟶ **HOLOGRAPH**

MARBLE ⟶ **STONES**

MARCASITE ⟶ **STONES**

MARIE-JEANNE ⟶ **BOTTLE SIZES**

MARQUETRY   Making of a decorated surface in furniture by the inlaying or embedding in a solid board or the application to it as a **VENEER** of a curvilinear pattern in woods of different kinds and colours. ⟶ **PARQUETRY**

MARQUISE CUT ⟶ **GEM CUTS**

MARVER   A polished slab of marble or iron on which glassblowers roll and mould the glass while it is still in a plastic condition and attached to the blow-pipe.

MAUCHLINE WARE   Early nineteenth-century wooden ware,

such as trinket boxes, decorated with tartan, or sometimes black and white, patterns. It takes its name from the Scottish town of Mauchline in Ayrshire, though it was made in many other places.

MAZER Originally a hard wood used for making drinking cups, the word has now taken the meaning of a bowl, drinking-cup, or goblet without a foot. Though this was originally of course made of mazer wood, the term is now often used for a bowl entirely of metal. ⟶ **TREEN**

MEDALLION In decorative work an oval, a circle, or a panel resembling a large medal.

MEDIUM Paper size⟶ Tables I and II

MEERSCHAUM A soft white stone (hydrous silicate of magnesium) occurring in clay-like masses and easily carved. A popular synonym for sepiolite. By extension, a tobacco pipe with a meerschaum bowl.

MEI P'ING ⟶ **CHINESE TERMS**

METAL (1) Molten **GLASS**

(2) ⟶ **ALLOY**

METHUSELAH ⟶ **BOTTLE SIZES**

METRIC SYSTEM ⟶ **WEIGHTS**

MEZZO RELIEVO/RILIEVO ⟶ **RELIEF**

MEZZOTINT ⟶ **PRINT**

MIDDLE RELIEF ⟶ **RELIEF**

MIHRAB The arch or niche at the top of the **FIELD** of a (Muslim) prayer rug.

MILLEFIORI Ornamental glass, usually found embedded in glass paper weights, formed by fusing together a bundle of glass rods or canes of different colours, generally drawing these to reduce the diameter of the bundle, which thus retains the pattern throughout its length, and then cutting into short sections used to build up a design.

MINION ⟶ **TYPE SIZES** (Table VI)

MIRAGE SET ⟶ **GEM SETTINGS**

MISERICORD A shelving projection on the underside of a hinged seat in a choir stall which gives support to one standing in the stall when the seat is turned up. Frequently rustically and entertainingly carved.

MITRE ⟶ **VESTMENT**

MIXED CUT ⟶ **GEM CUTS**

MOLIONET A swizzle stick

MODILLION A projecting bracket under the corona, itself a part with a broad vertical face, of a cornice in Corinthian and other **ORDERS**.

MONSTRANCE In the Roman Catholic church, (1) an open or transparent vessel of gold or silver in which the host is exposed, or (2) a receptacle for the exhibition of religious relics.

MONTEITH A punch-bowl with a scalloped rim on which to hang punch bowls or glasses. Said to be named after a 'Monsieur Monteith'. Term used from the end of the seventeenth century.

MOONSTONE ⟶ **STONES**

MORGANITE ⟶ **STONES**

MORION ⟶ **STONES**

MOROCCO LEATHER Leather made – originally, of course, in Morocco – from goatskins tanned with sumac. Applied also to an imitation of this made from sheep and lamb skins.

MOTHER-OF-PEARL ⟶ **STONES**

N

NACRE The smooth shiny iridescent substance forming the lining of many shells; mother-of-pearl.

NASHIJI A technique in the making of lacquer ware in which flakes of gold or silver foil are embedded at different levels in the lacquer.

NAVETTE-CUT ⟶ **GEM CUTS**

NEBUCHADNEZZAR ⟶ **BOTTLE SIZES**

NEGLIGEÉ Not only a lady's lighter and more informal garments, but also a necklace of irregular beads.

NEPHRITE ⟶ **STONES**

NETSUKE The toggle by which articles, particularly *INRO* and tobacco boxes or pouches, are attached to the belt in Japanese dress. Most commonly of ivory or bone, they are also frequently of wood or metal, and are generally most delicately carved in a multiplicity of naturalistic forms, and are perfect miniature works of art themselves.

NEWEL The pillar or post from which the steps of a winding staircase radiate. By extension, the post at the top or bottom of a staircase which supports the handrail.

NIELLO $\longrightarrow$ **ALLOY**

NIEN HAO $\longrightarrow$ **CHINESE TERMS**

NON PAREIL $\longrightarrow$ **TYPE SIZES**

NOTAPHILY An ugly new word meaning the collection of specimens of paper money.

O

OAK $\longrightarrow$ **WOODS**

OBELISK (1) A tapering shaft of stone, square or rectangular in section, with a pyramidal top.

(2) In modern printing used for † (dagger) mark which indicates footnotes, etc.

OBSIDIAN $\longrightarrow$ **GLASS**

OBUS CUT $\longrightarrow$ **GEM CUTS**

OBVERSE That side of a coin or medal on which the head or principal design is shown, the front; the opposite side, or back, being the **REVERSE**.

OCTAVO $\longrightarrow$ **BOOK SIZES**

OCTODECIMO $\longrightarrow$ **BOOK SIZES**

OGEE A shape or moulding consisting of a single double curve which in cross-section resembles the letter S, the upper half being convex and the lower concave. $\longrightarrow$ **CYMA**.

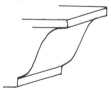

OJIME The small perforated round bead or button sliding on the suspension cords of an *INRO* to keep the latter tightly closed. Of many materials, they are often elegantly incised or decorated.

OLIPHANT A horn of ivory.

OLIVINE $\longrightarrow$ **STONES**

ONYX $\longrightarrow$ **STONES**

OPAL $\longrightarrow$ **STONES**

OPALINE (1) Semi-translucent glass; milk-glass.

(2) Of French coloured glass, a red tint known as *'gorge de pigeon'*, the most sought-after of colours.

OR $\longrightarrow$ **HERALDIC TERMS**

ORDER A system of parts subject to a uniformity of proportions, especially in classical architecture, whereby the types, particularly in relation to columns and their decoration, are prescribed. By extension the categories are extended to non-architectural subjects, such as **PLATE** and furniture. The principal orders, with the distinguishing features of their columns are, in order of historical appearance:

DORIC smooth column, resting on square base, crowned with capital consisting of ring of larger diameter beneath square **ENTABLATURE**.

IONIC **FLUTED** column characterized by two lateral **VOLUTES** of the capital.

CORINTHIAN **FLUTED** column characterized by capital with rows of **ACANTHUS** leaves.

TUSCAN smooth column devoid of all ornament.

COMPOSITE the grafting of the **CORINTHIAN** on the **IONIC** and thus a **FLUTED** column with capital incorporating both **VOLUTES** and **ACANTHUS** leaves. $\longrightarrow$ page 71

ORDINARY $\longrightarrow$ **HERALDIC TERMS**

ORMOLU $\longrightarrow$ **ALLOY**

ORPHREY (ORFRAY) Ornamental stripes and borders of ecclesiastical vestments, often richly embroidered.

ORRERY A clockwork mechanism to represent the move-

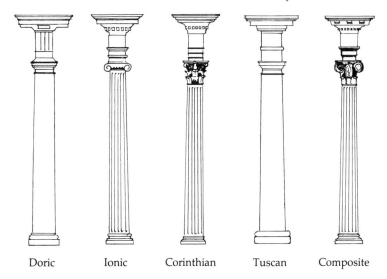

| Doric | Ionic | Corinthian | Tuscan | Composite |

ments of the planets round the sun (first made for the Earl of Orrery). Dates from the early eighteenth century.

ORRIS Lace of various patterns made in gold and silver; embroidery made in gold lace.

OVIFORM An auction catalogue's genteel way of saying 'egg-shaped'.

OVOLO A quarter-round moulding.

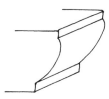

OYSTER-SHELL Of woods, particularly **WALNUT**, having circular markings reminiscent of the open shell of an oyster. Used in **VENEERS** for its decorative value. Obtained from transverse cutting of the small branches of the tree.

P **PADOUK (WOOD)** $\longrightarrow$ **WOODS**

PAKTONG $\longrightarrow$ **ALLOY**

PA KUA $\longrightarrow$ **CHINESE TERMS**

PALISANDER $\longrightarrow$ **WOODS**

PALLET In a clock, the steel surfaces which interrupt the passage of the cogs of the **SCAPEWHEEL**, giving impulse to the balance or pendulum.

PALMETTE Stylized ornament based on the leaf of the palm tree.

PALE $\longrightarrow$ **HERALDIC TERMS**

PA PAO $\longrightarrow$ **CHINESE TERMS**

PAPIER MÂCHÉ Though the words are French, the term is not of French origin (cf. **EPERGNE**). Pulped paper, moulded and dried, to make boxes, trays, etc. Usually painted a glossy black, and decorated with coloured painting. Sometimes inlaid with **MOTHER-OF-PEARL**.

PARAGON $\longrightarrow$ **TYPE SIZES**

PARCEL-GILT Partly gilded; especially of silver vessels, gilded, for example, on the inside.

PARCHMENT The skin of the sheep or goat prepared for writing, painting, etc. Whence **PARCHMENT PAPER**, that is, ordinary unglazed paper soaked in dilute sulphuric acid to produce a substance resembling real skin parchment.

PARGETING (or **PARGET**) Ornamental work in plaster and therefore frequently a facing in plaster, ornamented in **RELIEF** or **INTAGLIO**, decorating walls.

PARIAN MARBLE $\longrightarrow$ **STONES**

PARISON The rounded lump of molten glass which is first taken from a glass furnace and rolled before blowing begins.

PARQUETRY Making of a decorated surface, usually a floor, by the arrangement of rectilinear pieces of wood, often but not necessarily of different kinds and colours, in a pattern.
$\longrightarrow$ **MARQUETRY**

PARTI-BENDY $\longrightarrow$ **HERALDIC TERMS**

PARTNERS' TABLE A large flat writing table ($\longrightarrow$ **BUREAU**

PLAT) at which two persons could be seated side by side.

PARURE   A set of matching jewels intended to be worn together. Typically, a necklace, pair of earrings, a brooch, two bracelets, and a ring.

PASSANT ⟶ **HERALDIC TERMS**

PASTE   A hard vitreous composition of fused silica, potash, white oxide of lead, borax etc. (and therefore not unlike glass) used in making imitations of precious stones; when colourless and transparent particularly applied to imitation **DIAMONDS** (which do not pretend to be anything but imitation); whence paste jewellery.

PASTEL   A kind of dry paste made by compounding ground pigments with gum arabic to bind them, used as a medium for coloured drawings. By extension, pastel colours are soft colours.

PASTICHE   A (literary, musical, or other) work of art composed in the style of a well-known creator or artist.

PASTIGLIA   Coming, as the name implies, from Italy, it was a **STUCCO**-like substance used to make ornaments, particularly on picture frames from Venice in the fourteenth and fifteenth centuries. Usually gilded or painted.

PATEN   Shallow dish, usually round and of silver, on which the bread is laid in the celebration of the Eucharist. Hence a shallow dish or plate recalling this.

PATERA (pl. **PATERAE**)   A Roman patera having been a broad flat saucer or dish, the word has progressed to mean an ornament resembling a shallow dish, and thence to its commonest modern meaning of any flat round ornament in **BAS-RELIEF**.

PATINA   A film produced on the surface of old bronze, usually green, by the oxidation of the metal. Hence extended to similar changes in the surfaces of other substances.

PATINATION   The formation of a **PATINA**.

PAVÉ **SET** ⟶ **GEM SETTINGS**

PAVILION ⟶ **GEM CUTS**

PEACH BLOOM ⟶ **CERAMIC COLOURS**

PEARL (1) ⟶ **STONES**
       (2) ⟶ **TYPE SIZES** (Table VI)

PEARL WARE A white earthenware containing a greater percentage of flint and white clay than the softer cream-coloured earthenware.

PEDIMENT The triangular part, like a low gable, crowning a row of columns in classical Greek architecture. Also found in segmental form.

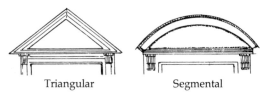

Triangular   Segmental

PEMBROKE TABLE A table on four fixed legs having two flaps which can be spread out horizontally to enlarge the table, supported by brackets connected to the central part by hinged joints. The term has been in use since the mid-eighteenth century.

PENDELOQUE-CUT ⟶ **GEM CUTS**

PENNER A pen-case; occasionally, a writing-case.

PENTELIC MARBLE ⟶ **STONES**

PERIDOT ⟶ **STONES**

PERNAMBUCO WOOD ⟶ **WOODS**

PETIT POINT ⟶ **STITCHES**

PETUNTSE ⟶ **CERAMICS**

PEWTER ⟶ **ALLOY**

Plate · 71

PICA $\longrightarrow$ **TYPE SIZES**

PICTOGRAM (PICTOGRAPH) A pictorial symbol or sign; a writing or record consisting of pictorial symbols. $\longrightarrow$ **IDEOGRAM**

PIE-CRUST EDGE A carved scalloped raised rim round the edge of a table, etc.

PILASTER A square or rectangular column or pillar, often fluted; frequently a fraction of such a pillar against, or forming part of, a wall.

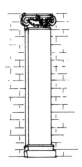

PINCHBECK $\longrightarrow$ **ALLOY**

PINCHER A glass stopper, e.g. for the bottles of a cruet stand.

PINEAPPLE Stylized forms of the pineapple, often found decorating gateposts, or as finials, were regarded as a symbol of hospitality.

PIPECLAY $\longrightarrow$ **CERAMICS**

PIQUÉ Ornamental work in tortoiseshell, enamel, etc. formed by minute inlaid designs traced in points of gold, etc.

PLATE A tiresome word, because it is not always clear from the context whether it means a collection of articles (table and other domestic ware) made of silver (from Spanish, *plata*) and gold; or whether it means articles made of baser metal and covered with a thin layer (or plate) of silver.

  ELECTRO-PLATE A form of silver **PLATE** in which the thin layer of silver has been applied to the base metal by electrolysis.

E.P.N.S. ELECTRO-PLATED NICKEL SILVER, nickel silver being an **ALLOY** and closely resembling **GERMAN SILVER**.

SHEFFIELD PLATE   A form of silver **PLATE** in which a thin film of **SILVER** is applied to copper, by a process, discovered in Sheffield, of fusing a thin billet of silver to a thicker one of copper and rolling the result.

PLATINUM ⟶ **ALLOY**

PLINTH   The square lowest part of a column or pedestal.

POINTILLISM (*POINTILLISME*)   The technique of certain French impressionist painters, known therefore as **POINTILLISTS** (*POINTILLISTES*), whereby the entire painting was executed in dots or **STIPPLES**, which are blended by the eye to form a pattern.

POLE SCREEN ⟶ **BANNER STAND**

POLYPTYCH   Anything consisting of more than three leaves folded together. ⟶ **DIPTYCH**, **TRIPTYCH**

POMANDER   A mixture of aromatic substances usually made into a ball to be carried on the person as a safeguard against infection or evil smells. Whence the case, usually a hollow ball, in which the substance was contained and carried. ⟶ **POUNCET-BOX, VINAIGRETTE**

POMMEL   The knob terminating the hilt of a sword or dagger.

PONTIL   An iron rod used for handling soft glass whilst it is being fashioned; also a coarse clay pipe used to support **CERAMIC** wares when being fired in the oven.

PORCELAIN ⟶ **CERAMICS**

PORPHYRY ⟶ **STONES**

PORRINGER   A small basin or similar vessel, with a flat handle at the edge, from which soup, porridge, children's food etc. is eaten. It is hardly to be distinguished from a **CAUDLE-CUP** or a **POSSET-CUP**, a caudle being a warm drink or thin gruel given to the sick and to their visitors, and a posset being a drink of hot milk curdled with ale, wine, etc. and spiced, and used as a delicacy or as a specific against colds.

POSSET CUP ⟶ **PORRINGER**

POST Paper size⟶ Tables I and II
POTATO RING ⟶ **DISH RING**
POTT Paper size⟶ Table 1
POTTERY ⟶ **CERAMICS**
POUNCE (1) Finely ground pumice, or fine sand, properly, mixed with powdered gum sandarac, used before the days of blotting paper to dry ink; whence the presence of a **POUNCE-POT** on many an early inkstand.

(2) To emboss metal work decoratively by raising the surface with blows struck from behind. ⟶ *REPOUSSÉ*
POUNCE-POT ⟶ **POUNCE**
POUNCET-BOX A small box with perforated lid for perfumes. ⟶ **POMANDER, VINAIGRETTE**
PRICKET Spike for impaling a candle on a candlestick, particularly a large candlestick as used on an altar.
PRIE-DIEU (1) A praying or kneeling desk.

(2) A chair with a tall sloping back for praying.
PRINT A picture made by printing from a block, the characteristic distinguishing a print from a drawing being the possibility of producing a vast number, which depends only on the wearing qualities of the block, of identical pictures. There are several methods, listed below, of making a print, which produce reproductions of different qualities. Most depend on creating grooves in a flat plate in which ink is held; the surface of the plate is wiped clean, and it is then pressed against the paper to which the ink is transferred. Some methods, however, leave the design in relief and this is inked and an impression transferred to the paper. For the most part prints are monochrome and are subsequently coloured by hand, if required, with water colours. But by using more than one block, each representing different parts of the picture, and different coloured inks, it is possible by making successive impressions on the same sheet of paper to produce polychrome prints.

AQUATINT **ETCHING** on copper making use of a resinous solution and nitric acid, which produces results resembling those of drawing in Indian ink or water colours. The print so made.

COLLOTYPE A **PRINT** made from a plate of which the printing surface is a thin film of gelatine which has been etched by the action of light. One of the most difficult forms of printing, capable of producing only a limited number of reproductions because of the fragile nature of the gelatine.

DRY-POINT (ENGRAVING) **ENGRAVING** made with a fine sharp pointed needle cutting directly into the flat copper plate which becomes the printing block.

ENGRAVING The generic word, when the incisions in the block, which can be of metal, stone, or wood, are made with coarser tools than a **DRY-POINT** needle.

ETCHING In this technique, where the printing block can only be of metal, the surface of the plate is covered with a protective film, e.g. wax, known as the **ETCHING-GROUND**; the design is cut through the etching-ground and the metal thus exposed is eaten away by acid to produce an etched plate. The print from such a plate is an etching.

HALF-TONE BLOCK The commonest method of reproducing photographs for printing. The photograph is divided into a grid of very fine squares, reproduced on metal, and the required shades or tones are achieved by etching away more or less of the infinite number of square dots to which the picture has been reduced by the grid.

LINO-CUT A very simple form of block in which a piece of linoleum is used as the block; the unwanted parts are cut away and the design is left in relief.

LITHOGRAPH A print where the block has been prepared by engraving on stone, usually a special quality of limestone or slate. When a coloured print is produced from several lithographic stones it is known as a **LITHOTINT**.

LITHOTINT ⟶ **LITHOGRAPH**

MEZZOTINT A method of **ENGRAVING** on steel or copper in which the surface of the plate is first roughened uniformly; the lights and half lights are then produced by scraping away the rough 'nap' so formed, the unscraped parts giving the densest colouring when a print is made. The print so made.

WOODBLOCK PRINT   A print from a block or blocks made of wood. Polychrome woodblock printing has been taken to a particularly advanced form of art by Japanese artists.

PROOF   (1) A coin or medal struck as the test of the die; also, one of a limited number of early impressions of a coin struck as specimens (appearing often as **PROOF SET** of a new issue of currency), especially from highly polished **FLANS**.

(2) An impression taken by an engraver from his block or plate to study the progress of his work; frequently now one of an arbitrary number of careful prints from the finished block, usually before the inscription is added.

PRUNT   A piece of ornamental glass laid upon a body of glass; hence the tool with which this is applied or moulded.

PUNTY (PONTY)   Iron rod or pipe used in glass-blowing; whence **PUNTY-MARK**, the mark left on blown glass at the point where the blow pipe is severed from the completed form. ⟶ **PONTIL**

PURDONIUM   Auction cataloguese for coal box. A Mr Purdon thought of fitting a removable metal lining to a coal box to simplify re-filling.

PURPLEWOOD ⟶ **WOODS**

PUSH-UP ⟶ **KICK**

PUTTO (pl. *PUTTI*)   Representation of children, usually boys and usually naked, particularly in painting and carving. ⟶ **AMORINO**

PYRIFORM   A word for the erudite who find pear-shaped too simple.

PYROPE GARNET ⟶ **STONES**

QUAICH (QUAIGH)   A shallow drinking cup, from Scotland, having two small ears or handles.

Q

QUARTER ⟶ **HERALDIC TERMS**

QUARTO ⟶ **BOOK SIZES**
QUARTZ ⟶ **STONES**
QUILLON = **POMMEL**

R **RAISED WORK** ⟶ **STUMPWORK**
RAMPANT ⟶ **HERALDIC TERMS**
RATTAN The name of several species of climbing palm, mostly from the East Indies, whose thin tough fibrous and pliable stems are used for walking canes and in the manufacture of cane furniture; in fabricated form usually a whitish yellow.

REEDED Ornamented with reed-moulding, a thin semi-cylindrical moulding reminiscent of the stem of the reed.

REGARDANT ⟶ **HERALDIC TERMS**

REGALIA The emblems or insignia of royalty – crown, orb, sceptre; by extension, the emblems or insignia of an order of chivalry or knighthood.

REGULATOR CLOCK ⟶ **CLOCKS**

REGULUS Purer or metallic part of a mineral separated by sinking to bottom in crucible.

REHOBOAM ⟶ **BOTTLE SIZES**

RELIEF In the plastic arts the elevation of a design from a flat surface to give a natural and solid appearance, the degree to which it projects, and the parts which project. The word is also used to describe the appearance of solidity which is given to a design on a flat surface by suitable use of the lines and colours of which the design is composed. Italian and French terms are freely used for the following categories of relief:

> **HIGH RELIEF** (Ital. *ALTO RELIEVO/RILIEVO*) In which the figures project more than half their thickness from the background.

> **LOW RELIEF** (Ital. *BASSO RELIEVO/RILIEVO*; Fr. *BAS-RELIEF*) In which the figures stand out less than half their true proportions from the background.

MIDDLE RELIEF (Ital. *MEZZO RELIEVO/RILIEVO*)   In which the figures stand out exactly half their true proportions from the background.

REPLICA   A copy, duplicate, **FACSIMILE**, or reproduction of a work of art. Strictly a replica, unlike the other words, means a copy made by the original artist. But modern usage is getting careless about this precise distinction.

REPOUSSÉ   Of metal work, raised into **RELIEF**, or ornamented in **RELIEF**, by being beaten or hammered from the reverse side.

REREDOS   A facing or screen of stone or wood covering the wall behind an altar; a hanging of silk or velvet for the same purpose: sometimes used for a choir screen.

RESEDA   A pale green colour similar to that of mignonette.

RESERVE   Of a design or pattern, an area set aside for special treatment distinct from the remainder.

RETABLE   A shelf or ledge on which ornaments may be placed; or, a frame enclosing decorated panels, above the back of an altar.

RETICULATE   To divide, mark, or ornament in such a way as to resemble network.

RETICULE   A small bag, usually of woven material, for carrying over the arm or in the hand.

REVERSE ⟶ **OBVERSE**

RHODONITE ⟶ **STONES**

RINCEAUX   Spirals of foliage as a decorative motif.

RING VELVET ⟶ **TEXTILES**

RIVIÈRE   A necklace, particularly of diamonds, and particularly of more than one strand, seen in the mind's eye as a flowing river.

RIZA   The plate covering an **ICON**, perforated to reveal the head of the saint portrayed.

ROBIN'S EGG BLUE ⟶ **CERAMIC COLOURS**

ROCAILLE   The representation of pebbles and, particularly, rough and asymmetric, rocks as ornamentation or background to a design. The word **ROCOCO** may be derived from the same stem.

ROCK CRYSTAL (CRISTAL) ⟶ **STONES**

ROCOCO Particularly of furniture or architecture, characterized by conventional shell- and scroll-work and florid ornamentation typical of the French workmanship under Louis XIV and XV. Whence, excessively ornate.

ROLL-TOP DESK One having a **TAMBOUR** closure moving from front to back.

RÖMER ⟶ **RUMMER**

ROSE CUT ⟶ **GEM CUTS**

ROSE QUARTZ ⟶ **STONES**

ROTTEN-STONE ⟶ **TRIPOLI**

ROUGE DE FER ⟶ **IRON-RED**

ROUNDEL A decorative plate or panel, round in shape.

ROYAL Paper size ⟶ Tables I and II

RUBY (1) ⟶ **STONES**

   (2) ⟶ **TYPE SIZES** (Table VI)

RUMMER A drinking glass of goblet shape. Originally of green glass from the Rhineland, their name was **RÖMER**: this became perverted in English. Again originally the bowl was a cut-off sphere and the stem, decorated with **PRUNT**s, was conical, expanding towards the bottom, with ribbing formed by winding glass rod spirally over a conical form. Nowadays the vessel has bowls of varied shapes, a squat stem, and sometimes even a square foot. They are characteristically thick and heavy.

S **SABICU** ⟶ **WOODS**

SABLE ⟶ **HERALDIC TERMS**

SAGGAR A vessel of already baked fire-proof clay on which, or within which, finer articles of **PORCELAIN** are placed for protection prior to firing in the kiln.

SALMANAZER ⟶ **BOTTLE SIZES**

SALT GLAZE ⟶ **CERAMICS**

SALTIRE ⟶ **HERALDIC TERMS**

SALVER Originally a tray on which food or drink was placed after it had been shown to be safe (Latin, *salvus* = safe) to consume, the word now means simply tray for serving food, presenting letters etc.

SANDALWOOD $\longrightarrow$ **WOODS**

SANG DE BOEUF $\longrightarrow$ **CERAMIC COLOURS**

SANGUINE   A crayon coloured red with iron oxide; a drawing executed in red chalks.

SANSERIF (SANS-SERIF)   A printed letter without **SERIF**.

SAN TO $\longrightarrow$ **CHINESE TERMS**

SAN TS'AI $\longrightarrow$ **CHINESE TERMS**

SAPPHIRE $\longrightarrow$ **STONES**

SARDONYX $\longrightarrow$ **STONES**

SATIN $\longrightarrow$ **TEXTILES**

SATINWOOD $\longrightarrow$ **WOODS**

SAUTOIR   A necklace.

SAXON MONEYER'S POUND $\longrightarrow$ **WEIGHTS**

SCAGLIOLA   A marble substitute of plaster of Paris and glue incorporating chips of marble. Polishes well.

SCAPEWHEEL   The last wheel in the **GOING TRAIN** of a clock or watch that operates the **ESCAPEMENT**.

SCARAB   By reference to the scarab beetle reverenced by the ancient Egyptians, a gem-stone cut in the form of a beetle, having a design in **INTAGLIO** on the underside.

SCONCE   A bracket candlestick that is set upon a wall, generally with a reflecting surface at the point where it is attached to the wall. Sconces date from the second half of the seventeenth century. A rarer use is for the tube or socket in which the candle is set in an ordinary candlestick.

SCOTIA MOULDING   Half-round concave moulding, originally between two **TORUS** mouldings. Reverse of **ASTRAGAL**.

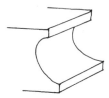

SCUTCHEON = ESCUTCHEON (1)

SCRIM $\longrightarrow$ **TEXTILES**

SCRIMSHAW A generic term for the handwork, such as the carving of bone and ivory, carried out by sailors to beguile the time on long sailing-ship voyages.

SEAL CUT $\longrightarrow$ **GEM CUTS**

SECRETAIRE A piece of furniture for keeping papers in, either in drawers or a cupboard below, and for writing, usually with a forward folding flap and having pigeon-holes within. A **BUREAU**. Perhaps most commonly used in the term **SECRETAIRE-BOOKCASE** when a section with doors, frequently glazed, and shelves is added above.

SEED PEARL $\longrightarrow$ **STONES**

SEHNA (or SENNEH) KNOT Knot, originally of Persian origin, used in making hand-made oriental carpets.

SEJANT $\longrightarrow$ **HERALDIC TERMS**

SENNEH KNOT $\longrightarrow$ **SEHNA KNOT**

SEQUIN Nowadays mostly thought of as a small spangle used to adorn garments, it remains for the numismatist the anglicized name of the small Venetian gold coin, the *ZECCHINO*, named after the mint in Venice, the *Zecca*. The word *zecca* itself is derived from the Arabic word for a die used in coining.

SERIF The small cross-line that embellishes the end of a stroke in a printed letter.

SERPENTINE (1) In cabinet making, having a symmetrical curving shape, suggesting the sinuosities of a serpent. Generally applied to curved-fronted articles.

(2) $\longrightarrow$ **STONES**

SETTEE $\longrightarrow$ **COUCH**

SETTLE $\longrightarrow$ **COUCH**

SEXTO DECIMO $\longrightarrow$ **BOOK SIZES**

SHAGREEN Untanned leather with a rough granular surface prepared from the skin of horse, donkey, shark, etc., and often dyed green. Originally spelled 'chagrin'.

SHAKUDO $\longrightarrow$ **ALLOY**

SHANK   In addition to being the straight part, in some way reminiscent of a leg, of a great many common articles, it is that curved part of a ring which surrounds the finger.

SHEFFIELD PLATE $\longrightarrow$ **PLATE**

SHELLAC   **LAC** melted, strained, and formed into thin plates. $\longrightarrow$ **FRENCH POLISH**

SHIBAYAMA   A technique in the making of ornamental lacquer ware in which pieces of ivory, tortoiseshell, and mother-of-pearl are placed in the lacquer to help build up a picture. Named after the Japanese inventor of the technique.

SHIBUICHI $\longrightarrow$ **ALLOY**

SHOU $\longrightarrow$ **CHINESE TERMS**

SHOULDER   Of a gem-set ring, the space on either side of the stone between the setting and the **SHANK**.

SIGHT SIZE   Of a framed picture, the dimensions of the visible portion.

SILVER $\longrightarrow$ **ALLOY**

SILVER-GILT   Gilded silver. $\longrightarrow$ **WATER-GILDING, PARCEL-GILT**

SILVER POINT DRAWING   The process of making a drawing with a silver pencil on specially prepared paper.

SINISTER $\longrightarrow$ **HERALDIC TERMS**

SIXTEENMO $\longrightarrow$ **BOOK SIZES**

SKILLET   A metal cooking vessel having three or four feet and a long handle; loosely, a saucepan or stewpan.

SKIVE   The wheel on which a diamond is polished to produce facets. $\longrightarrow$ **GEM CUTS**

SKIVER   A thin kind of dressed leather, split from the outside of a sheepskin, tanned in sumach, and used for bookbinding, the covering of flat surfaces of furniture, etc.

SLIP $\longrightarrow$ **CERAMICS**

SMALL PICA $\longrightarrow$ Table VI

SMOKEY QUARTZ $\longrightarrow$ **STONES**

SNAPHAUNCE   An early form of **FLINT-LOCK** for muskets and pistols; whence the weapon fitted with such a lock.

SNUFFER   (1) An instrument for removing the snuff, or

charred portion of the wick, of a candle. As it is of scissor-like construction it is usually called a pair of snuffers.

(2) A metal cone for snuffing out, or extinguishing, a candle flame by covering it.

SOAPSTONE ⟶ **STONES**

SOCLE A low plain block or plinth serving as a pedestal for a statue, etc.

SODA GLASS ⟶ **GLASS**

SOFA ⟶ **COUCH**

SOFA TABLE A long narrow table with short folding flaps at each end, conceived to be placed along the back of a **SOFA**.

SOFT PASTE ⟶ **CERAMICS**

SPANISH MAHOGANY ⟶ **WOODS**

SPANDREL The triangular space between the curve of an arch and the rectangle formed by the moulding enclosing it; any similar space between an arch and the straight-sided figure bounding it.

SPHENE ⟶ **STONES**

SPINEL ⟶ **STONES**

SPLAT A board, bar, etc., forming the centre part, within the frame, of the back of a chair.

SPLINE A long, narrow, and relatively thin piece or strip of wood, metal, etc. Used of the back of a book.

SPLITS Decoration consisting of closely spaced vertical cuts around the foot of a decanter, to hide the sediment of the wine.

SQUAB A (generally) thin (though the dictionary will tell you thick) cushion laid on a board or cane seat to protect, re-spectively, the human or the cane seat.

STANDING CUP   Particularly of oriental porcelain, wide and shallow saucer-like cup fixed to the top of a tall conical stem. Also known as a **STEM CUP**.

STANDING SALT   ⟶ **CELLAR**

STANDISH   The usual name until the beginning of the nine-teenth century for an inkstand.

STATANT   ⟶ **HERALDIC TERMS**

STEELYARD   A balance for weighing, consisting of a metal bar (a yard of steel) with a fulcrum near one end. The object to be weighed is attached to the short arm and a counter weight is moved along the notched and graduated longer arm until equilibrium is reached and the weight read off the scale.

STEM CUP = **STANDING CUP**

STEP CUT   ⟶ **GEM CUTS**

STERLING   A standard of purity for silver ware, meaning a minimum content of 92.5 per cent (925 millesimes) pure silver in the **ALLOY**.

STIPPLE   Stipples are small spots or dots used in painting, **ENGRAVING**, etc. to produce gradations of shadings.

STITCHES   In **BERLIN WOOLWORK** or other embroidery on canvas the three commonest stitches are:

  CROSS STITCH   As its name implies, two stitches at right angles over the crossing point of the threads of the canvas.

  GROS POINT   One half of the cross of **CROSS STITCH**.

  PETIT POINT (**TENT STITCH**)   The same as **GROS POINT**, but worked with a finer (generally single) thread on a finer canvas.

STOLE   ⟶ **VESTMENT**

STONES   Some purists argue that there are only five 'real' gemstones – diamond, emerald, ruby, sapphire, and pearl. They acknowledge in the same breadth that the last – pearl – is not a stone at all. So much for their 'purity'.

  Any number of stones occurring in nature have, when suitably cut and polished, such attractive colours and reflections that they are used in jewellery and, in the case of the more easily found, and therefore cheaper, stones, for the making of larger decorative objects. Some are harder and more durable; others, softer, better lend themselves to plastic treatment, and are carved or sculpted. The rarer, generally translucent, coloured stones, mostly small in size, tend to be spoken of in general parlance as gemstones. The commoner, mainly opaque, larger stones tend to be referred to as hardstones. But some are not in fact particularly hard (e.g. alabaster). The curious might care to read the description of the breastplate of the Israelite High Priest in the thirty-ninth chapter of the Book of Exodus. Stones of identical chemical composition, or, alternatively, of basically identical composition but with minute differences, can have different colours and different names. To list them all, with an adequate distinguishing description of their chemical and crystalline structure is the business of a specialist geological or gemmological treatise. The list that follows seeks to do no more than describe some of the broad characteristics of the commoner forms of stones that are frequently found in jewellery, small carvings, and other decorative *objets d'art*, and in furniture; it does not pretend to be adequate to help a collector of mineral specimens.

AGATE   A hardstone, of wide colour range, mainly reds and browns, but can consist even of blacks and whites. Geologically, one of the semi-pellucid variegated chalcedonies, having the colours arranged in stripes or bands, or blended in clouds; whence **BANDED AGATE, RIBBON AGATE, MOSS AGATE**. Takes a high polish.

ALABASTER   A soft, generally white stone, but also found naturally in yellow, reddish, or clouded hues. Can be easily carved and dyed. Geologically a sulphate of lime, or gypsum. But the word is also used for carbonate of lime.

ALEXANDRITE   A very rare kind of **CHRYSOBERYL** found in the Ural mountains, and named after the Tsar Alexander.

Its peculiarity is that by daylight it is green, whereas by lamplight it turns red.

ALMANDINE GARNET ⟶ **GARNET**

AMBER   Not a natural mineral stone, but the petrified resin of pine trees. Ranges in colour from deep orange-red to pale yellow. The commonest source is the Baltic. As insects were sometimes trapped in the natural resin, a 'fly in amber' is much prized by some.

AMETHYST   A **QUARTZ**, coloured by manganese, or by a compound of iron and soda, ranging through all the tones of violet and purple, from pale to dark.

AQUAMARINE   A bluish-green variety of **BERYL**.

AVENTURINE QUARTZ   A variety of **QUARTZ** spangled with yellow scales of mica. The term derives from aventurine glass, a glass containing golden spangles, the technique for whose manufacture was discovered by accident.

BANDED AGATE ⟶ **AGATE**

BANDED JASPER ⟶ **JASPER**

BAROQUE PEARL ⟶ **PEARL**

BERYL   Chemically a silicate of aluminium and glucinum which crystallizes in hexagonal prisms, **BERYL** is a general term whose varieties include **EMERALD** and **AQUAMARINE**. Pink, yellow, and white varieties are found and known by the specialized names of **MORGANITE**, **HELIODORE**, and **GOSHENITE** respectively.

BLOODSTONE ⟶ **JASPER**

BUTTON PEARL ⟶ **PEARL**

CAIRNGORM   A yellow form of **QUARTZ**, which is properly called **CITRINE**, and for which **CAIRNGORM** is a local Scottish name. It is sometimes sold by jewellers as **TOPAZ**. It can be produced by heat treatment of pale **AMETHYSTS**.

CANARY DIAMOND ⟶ **DIAMOND**

CARBUNCLE   A name used for a **CABOCHON CUT ALMANDINE GARNET**. Purplish red.

CARNELIAN   The spelling preferred in the United States for what is correctly **CORNELIAN**.

CAT'S EYE   The name is given to brown versions of both **CHRYSOBERYL** and **QUARTZ** which, when presented in an oval **CABOCHON CUT**, show a reflected line of light along the long axis reminiscent of the slit iris of the eye of a cat.

CHALCEDONY   A version (for the specialist, a cryptocrystalline version) of **QUARTZ**. In its commonest form an opaque white of rather waxy appearance. **AGATES** include any chalcedony that shows a pattern.

CHRYSOPRASE   An apple-green translucent variety of **CHALCEDONY**.

CINNAMON DIAMOND $\longrightarrow$ **DIAMOND**

CINNAMON STONE = HESSONITE GARNET

CITRINE   A pale yellow variety of **QUARTZ**. $\longrightarrow$ **CAIRNGORM, JACINTH**

CORAL   Not a natural mineral stone at all but the skeleton of certain marine animals. To be found in many configurations and colours, principally white, pink, and red. The most solid, in branch-like form, is red, coming from the Red Sea and Mediterranean, and takes a high polish.

CORNELIAN   A variety of **CHALCEDONY**, semi-transparent, of glowing orange-red. Used for seals and such-like purposes.

CULTURED PEARL $\longrightarrow$ **PEARL**

DEMANTOID GARNET $\longrightarrow$ **GARNET**

DIAMOND   The hardest, not only stone, but substance known. In its commonest form white, translucent, having a high refracting property, so that when properly cut and faceted the most brilliant of all the gems. Chemically it is pure crystalline carbon. Diamonds have been made synthetically by exposing pure carbon to great heat and pressure, but the product has been only minute in size, with none of the brilliance of a gem diamond, and suitable only for use as an industrial diamond – that is, for its abrasive quality.

Rough diamonds, as mined, frequently contain impurities or flaws, and much must be cut away in the process of producing a pure gem. These cuttings are not wasted, being used for smaller gems, or industrial purposes.

Though most commonly white, sometimes tinged with blue, the natural diamond occurs in a range of colours from white to yellow which have their own special names, set out below in descending order of esteem and value.

The ideal is pure white, with a glimmer of blue; if a slightly smoky blue the quality is known as 'premier'. If tinged with yellow, known as CAPE, they are classified thus:

Top silver cape	*or*	Top light brown
Silver cape	*or*	Light brown
Light cape	*or*	Brown
Hard cape	*or*	Cinnamon

When the colour is deep brown it is known as CINNA-MON, and has little value. However, a diamond of a rich daffodil yellow is known as CANARY and is highly prized. Other colours are found, very rarely, and can be olive, aquamarine, pink, red, and sapphire blue. Some of these colours can be faked, either with indigo washes (to make yellowish stones white) or by exposure to atomic radiation (to produce yellows, blues, and greens).

In the United States a different vocabulary is used for the colours, as follows:

River	– Blue white
Top Wesselton	– Finest white
Wesselton	– White
Top crystal	– White, faintly tinted
Crystal	– White, tinted
Top Cape	– Slightly yellowish
Cape	– Yellowish
Light yellow	– Light yellow
Yellow	– Yellow

The purity of a diamond is judged by whether or not the stone contains natural inclusions and whether, if it does, these are sufficient to compromise its brilliance. Jewellers have a scale and vocabulary to classify this quality, just as they classify colour. The scale is based on what can be seen with a 10-power magnifier.

Pure	contains no visible inclusion
VVSI (very very small inclusions)	contains one or two inclusions, difficult even for an expert to detect
VSI (very small inclusions	contains several inclusions, also difficult to detect
SI (small inclusions)	contains inclusions which are easily visible
First piqué	contains quite clearly visible inclusions, which, however, do not spoil the brilliance of the stone and which cannot be seen with the naked eye

EMERALD   The most precious member of the BERYL family, is at its best when it is a vivid grass green, the colouring being due to traces of chromium. It is a hexagonal prism, and seldom without flaws, cracks, and fissures.

FIRE OPAL $\longrightarrow$ OPAL

FRESHWATER PEARL $\longrightarrow$ PEARL

GARNET   Derives its name from the supposed resemblance of its colour to the flesh of the pomegranate; therefore red – but in various shades, with individual names. Garnet is an oxide of aluminium, combined with other metals in varying proportions – calcium, iron, magnesium, etc. – and it is the variation in these proportions that gives the various colours. Was much mined in Bohemia in the eighteenth and nineteenth centuries and set in gold for jewellery (especially the PYROPE Garnet).

ALMANDINE GARNET   Is an oxide of iron and aluminium, with some magnesium. Of a violet or **AMETHYST** hue.

DEMANTOID GARNET   Is purplish red and when cut as a hollow **CABOCHON** is known as a **CARBUNCLE**.

GROSSULAR GARNET   Unlike most members of the garnet family, is not red, but a green translucent stone, often speckled with black, from South Africa and Siberia.

HESSONITE GARNET   Known also as **CINNAMON STONE**, and shares with **CITRINE** and **ZIRCON** the old name of **JACINTH**. Rich brown in colour.

PYROPE GARNET   A deep fiery red variant, usually cut with facets for jewellery.

GOSHENITE ⟶ **BERYL**

GROSSULAR GARNET ⟶ **GARNET**

HARDSTONE   A collective term, used particularly in auction catalogues, to lump together the less precious (and, obviously, harder) stones, in which artefacts of larger than conventional jewel size are carved; it can be found to include at least **AGATE**, **LAPIS LAZULI**, **OBSIDIAN**, **ONYX**, **ROCK CRYSTAL**, and **ROSE QUARTZ**: **JADE** tends to have separate mention in its own right (e.g. 'Jade and hard-stone objects'), perhaps because of the high esteem in which jade has always been held in the Orient, and in pre-Columbian America.

HELIODORE ⟶ **BERYL**

HESSONITE GARNET ⟶ **GARNET**

JACINTH ⟶ **CITRINE**, **ZIRCON**   Reddish-orange.

JADE   A term used to cover two quite different minerals, **JADEITE** and **NEPHRITE**.

JADEITE   A silicate of sodium and aluminium, it is the more valuable of the two, comes principally from Burma, and occurs in a wide variety of colours. Emerald green is the most prized variety but lavender, brown, red, white, and black also occur. Tough rather than hard.

NEPHRITE   A silicate of lime and magnesia, it is typically green in colour. It comes mainly from Siberia, Turkestan, and New Zealand. A dark green variety flecked with black is known as **SPINACH JADE** and an off-white variety as **MUTTON FAT JADE**.

JARGOON $\longrightarrow$ **ZIRCON**

JASPER **CHALCEDONY** adulterated with clayey material, usually red, yellow, or brown, due to the presence of iron oxide. The red is the most attractive. **BANDED JASPER** is striped with dull green and maroon. Dark green jasper with red spots in it is known as **BLOODSTONE**.

JET Very hard coal.

LAPIS LAZULI An opaque stone of deep blue colour, of complex chemical structure.

SWISS LAPIS **JASPER** stained blue.

MALACHITE An opaque stone of vivid green, supposedly resembling the green of the leaf of the mallow, often with whorls and striations of black and paler shades of green. A hydrous carbonate of copper. Comes especially from Russia.

MARBLE Limestone in a crystalline form; hard and capable of taking a high polish. The word probably conjures up first in the mind's eye the perfect white which Michelangelo used for his masterpieces and which came from the quarries of **CARRARA**. But marble is found in a very wide variety of colours and combinations, many of which have been given the names of the places or quarries whence they principally came, which names have then become descriptive of a particular colour or variegation.

BRECCIA A variegated marble of grey, black, yellow, and red.

CARRARA From Carrara in Italy; white.

PARIAN From the Greek island of Paros; white.

PENTELIC From Mount Pentelicus near Athens; white.

VERDE DI PRATO A greenish marble.

MARCASITE Faceted iron pyrites, used as a minor grey/black gemstone.

MOONSTONE   A translucent stone with a pearly lustre. A form of **FELDSPAR**. The best comes from Ceylon.

MORGANITE $\longrightarrow$ **BERYL**

MORION $\longrightarrow$ **SMOKEY QUARTZ**

MOTHER-OF-PEARL $\longrightarrow$ **PEARL**

NEPHRITE $\longrightarrow$ **JADE**

OBSIDIAN $\longrightarrow$ **GLASS**

OLIVINE   A variety of chrysolite, mainly olive-green in colour. As a gemstone, more usually known as **PERIDOT**, comes principally from the area of the Red Sea.

ONYX   A variety of **QUARTZ**. Black, often banded with white. Similar to **AGATE**.

OPAL   A form of hydrous silica somewhat resembling **QUARTZ**, sparkling and flashing in many colours depending on how the light falls on it. The play of colour comes from light interference, analogous to the iridescence of a soap bubble. The moisture in the stone, which causes the interference, will over long periods of time dry out; the stone will lose its colour and can crack. The most precious, **BLACK OPAL**, comes from Australia; **FIRE OPAL**, usually quite transparent, and orange in colour, comes from Mexico.

PEARL   Often known as the oriental pearl. As already noted, not a stone of mineral origin, but crystalline in structure. Formed in oysters and some other molluscs, by the envelopment, generally in spherical form, within the flesh of the mollusc, of a foreign body, with a layer of the same nacre as forms the lining of the mollusc's shell. Pearls, though generally white, can vary in hue, some being pink, and others black, which are highly prized.

BAROQUE PEARL   Any pearl of irregular shape.

BUTTON PEARL   (1) A pearl formed naturally not as a sphere, but as a domed round or oval disc.

(2) The iridescent nacreous lining of the shells of various molluscs, used for making ornamental buttons.

CULTURED PEARL Formed naturally by the oyster in response to the deliberate insertion by man in controlled conditions of a foreign body (a bead of freshwater mussel with a particle of mother-of-pearl attached) in the flesh of the oyster.

FRESHWATER PEARL Formed in some species of freshwater mussel, in the same way as the oriental pearl. Often of bizarre shapes.

MOTHER-OF-PEARL The smooth, shining, iridescent substance forming the lining of many shells. ⟶ BUTTON PEARL

SEED PEARL A minute natural pearl.

PERIDOT ⟶ OLIVINE

PORPHYRY A hard rock, capable of taking a high polish, in which red or white crystals are embedded in a deep red mass.

PYROPE GARNET ⟶ GARNET

QUARTZ Quartz in all its different forms is perhaps the stone most used in jewellery. It occurs either as hexagonal prisms or in massive form. In its purest form, it is silica or silicon dioxide, and is known as ROCK CRYSTAL (CRISTAL), the natural substance that it was the ambition of the glassmakers to imitate. Forms of quartz not mentioned elsewhere in this list which are frequently used in jewellery or *objets d'art* include:

ROSE QUARTZ A cloudy pink translucent stone.

SMOKY QUARTZ This is also called MORION. Is a dark molasses colour. ⟶ CAIRNGORM

RHODONITE A pink opaque stone with black markings, coming principally from the Ural Mountains.

ROCK CRYSTAL (CRISTAL). ⟶ QUARTZ

RUBY A translucent red variety of corundum (crystalline alumina), ranging from deep crimson to pale rose-red. The best come from Burma, but stones of good quality come also from Ceylon and Siam, the latter being brownish. All the other colour variants of corundum but red are known as **SAPPHIRES**. As the value of a ruby greatly exceeds that of a **SAPPHIRE** it is of more than academic interest at what point a pink sapphire becomes a ruby.

SAPPHIRE   The characteristic colour of the sapphire is a rich transparent blue; but there is a wide range of colours in stones that are true sapphires, for instance, pink, green, purple, and yellow. The best stones come from Kashmir, but high quality sapphires come also from Burma and Ceylon. ⟶ **RUBY**. Some sapphires, particularly when cut in **CABOCHON** form, exhibit within the stone an appearance of light in the shape of a six-rayed star; these are known as **STAR SAPPHIRES**.

SARDONYX   A variety of **ONYX** or stratified **CHALCEDONY** having white layers alternating with layers of a variety of **CORNELIAN** (known as sard) varying in colour from yellow to reddish orange.

SEED PEARL   ⟶ **PEARL**

SERPENTINE   A stone of a dull green colour with markings resembling those of a serpent's skin. Sometimes referred to as **SERPENTINE MARBLE**.

SMOKY QUARTZ   ⟶ **QUARTZ**

SOAPSTONE   A massive whitish form of talc, having a smooth greasy feel, which, being soft, is easily carved.

SPHENE   A very rare stone, green, yellow, or brown, of exceptional brilliance, from Switzerland.

SPINEL   A range of clear stones found in almost every colour; the red is known as ruby spinel.

SWISS LAPIS   ⟶ **LAPIS LAZULI**

TANZANITE   A gem stone, discovered only in the middle of this century, at a single site in Tanzania. It is a dark royal blue in colour, opaque rather than translucent, and though very elegant somewhat soft for a satisfactory gemstone.

TIGER'S EYE   A yellowish variety of **QUARTZ**, containing fibres of asbestos, which give it a golden-brown sheen.

TOPAZ   The typical colour is a sherry-brown, but colours as varied as blue, pink, and yellow are found. The best stones come from Brazil. The topaz takes a high polish and has a soapy feel, which distinguishes it from **CITRINE**.

TOURMALINE A mineral naturally occurring in long crystals, its commonest colours are dark green or pink. But almost any shade is possible.

TURQUOISE Turquoise originally came from Persia, but was shipped through Turkey, whence its name. Sky-blue in colour at its best, but can shade to green. Often minor pieces appear embedded in the natural rock in which it is found; these are known as **TURQUOISE MATRIX**.

ZIRCON Of old known as the **JACINTH** (or **HYACINTH**), the zircon occurs in all colours. It has great brilliance and lustre, so that the white zircon (or **JARGOON**) has tended to be passed off as a diamond substitute. Though fairly hard, it is brittle, so that facet edges get chipped. Red to brown stones are common.

STONEWARE ⟶ **CERAMICS**

STRAPWORK Ornament consisting of flat interlacing bands.

STRETCHER A bar or strut used as a tie or brace in the framework of an article, particularly a cross-piece between the legs of a chair or table.

STRIKING TRAIN ⟶ **TRAIN**

STRINGING Straight or curved inlaid lines in cabinet work.

STUCCO (1) A fine plaster, especially one composed of gypsum and pulverized marble, used for covering walls and ceilings and for making mouldings.

(2) A coarse plaster used for covering exterior surface of walls, in imitation of stone.

STUMP A cylinder of rolled paper or other material with conical ends, like a sharpened pencil, used for blurring the edges of pencil or pastel marks in drawing.

STUMPWORK A form of embroidery in relief, often with the figures padded, and properly called **RAISED WORK**.

SULPHIDE ⟶ *CRYSTALLO-CERAMIE*

SUPPORTER ⟶ **HERALDIC TERMS**

SWAG An ornament formed of a wreath or **FESTOON** of foliage, flowers, or fruit, fastened up at both ends and hanging down in the centre.

SWAGE An ornamental grooving, moulding, or border; a circular or semi-circular groove, for example on an anvil, by means of which cold metal is shaped.

SWISS LAPIS ⟶ **STONES**

SYCAMORE ⟶ **WOODS**

T

TABLE ⟶ **GEM CUTS**

TABLE CLOCK ⟶ **CLOCKS**

TABLE-CUT ⟶ **GEM CUTS**

TABLE DE CHEVET Bedside table (French *chevet* = pillow).

TAFFETA ⟶ **TEXTILES**

T'AI-PO TSUN ⟶ **CHINESE TERMS**

TALLBOY A tall chest of drawers, often raised on legs, and usually in two parts, made from the end of the seventeenth century. Sometimes used of a chest of drawers or bureau standing on a dressing table. In America frequently called **HIGHBOY.** ⟶ **LOWBOY**

TAMBOUR SHUTTER A flexible closure for desks, cabinets, etc. made by gluing strips of wood, inserted into a groove at each end, on linen or canvas.

TANKARD A drinking vessel, formerly of wooden staves and hooped, now especially a tall one-handled mug or jug, in various substances, particularly **PEWTER**, chiefly used for beer.

TANTONY This abbreviation of 'St Anthony' means a hand bell or small church bell (and, for the collector of words, it also means the smallest pig in a litter).

TANZANITE ⟶ **STONES**

T'AO T'IEH ⟶ **CHINESE TERMS**

TAPESTRY A textile in which the pattern is formed by coloured weft threads as they are woven into the warp, and are thus part of the fabric, which has no existence without them. To be distinguished from embroidery, which is the application of coloured threads to an already complete fabric.

TAZZA A shallow ornamental bowl or vase, properly one supported on a foot. ⟶ **STANDING CUP**

TEA CANDLESTICK Half-size editions of table candlesticks, of mid-eighteenth century.

TEA DUST ⟶ **CERAMIC COLOURS**

TEAPOY A three-legged table or stand. Has nothing to do with tea, except that such a table was a convenient stand for a tea-tray.

TEMPERA The method of painting in **DISTEMPER**.

TENT STITCH ⟶ **STITCHES**

TERM A statue or bust representing the upper part of the body sometimes without arms springing from a pedestal or pillar, the whole being used as a pillar.

TERRA-COTTA ⟶ **CERAMICS**

TERRINE ⟶ **TUREEN**

TESTER A canopy over a (four-poster) bed.

TEXTILES It would be a forlorn hope to try to include in a dictionary of this compass distinguishing descriptions of all woven textiles. The following brief notes are intended to be no more than signposts to recognition of a few of the fabrics more commonly met in articles of furniture or embroidery. ⟶ **TAPESTRY**

    BAIZE A coarse woollen cloth with a long nap, frequently used for table coverings and curtains.

    BROCADE A fabric now generally, but not necessarily, of silk, woven with a raised design, that was originally in threads of silver and gold.

    CHINTZ Glazed calico, printed in colours on a pale background.

    DAMASK (1) A rich silk fabric, originally produced at Damascus, woven with elaborate designs and figures.

        (2) A twilled linen fabric, used particularly for

table linen, where by the nature of the weaving, a pattern is shown up by different reflections of light from the surface.

GROSGRAIN (GROGRAM)   A stiff corded silk fabric.

SATIN   A silk fabric so woven that one side has a glossy surface.

SCRIM   Open-weave fabric, particularly of cotton, used for lining, upholstery, etc.

TAFFETA   A thin silk material of decided brightness or lustre.

VELVET   A silk fabric having a short compact and smooth piled surface. When the weft threads that are drawn through to produce the pile on one side are left uncut, it is known as RING VELVET. When the fabric is woven from cotton instead of silk, it is called VELVETEEN.

THERMOLUMINESCENCE TEST   A test for the antiquity of objects made from minerals, particularly CERAMIC wares; it depends on the quantity of light emitted when the material is heated, which is proportional to the time during which the object has stored energy from the ambient radiation. In the firing process of ceramic-making all such energy previously accumulated in the material is driven off, setting a time-zero directly related to the age of the object.

THIRTY-TWOMO ⟶ BOOK SIZES

THYRSUS   A staff or rod tipped with an ornament like a pine-cone.

TIARA   An ornamental, generally jewelled, coronet or head-band.

TIG ⟶ TYG

TIGER'S EYE ⟶ STONES

TIGER WARE   An early English term for stoneware jugs with a mottled glaze which were imported from the Rhineland.

TIMEPIECE   A technical term meaning a clock which does not strike.

TINCTURE ⟶ HERALDIC TERMS

TING ⟶ CHINESE TERMS

TIN GLAZE ⟶ **CERAMICS**

TONBRIDGE WARE A form of decoration consisting of **MARQUETRY** whose patterns are formed by immense numbers of very small squares of different coloured woods. The effect is an equivalent in woodwork to **CROSS-STITCH** in embroidery.

TONDO A painting or **RELIEF** of circular form.

TOOLING The impressing of designs on leather by heated tools or stamps; the design so formed, which is generally coloured, most commonly with gilding (**GOLD-TOOLING** or **GILT-TOOLING**) but need not be (**BLIND-TOOLING**).

TOPAZ ⟶ **STONES**

TORC (TORQUE) Necklace of twisted metal, particularly of the ancient Britons and Gauls.

TORCHÈRE A tall small-topped stand, on which to set a torch or lamp.

TORTOISESHELL The semi-transparent shell, mottled or variegated in shades of black, red, and yellow, of certain tortoises, which with heat can be moulded and takes a high polish. Used for making ornamental objects and in inlaying.

TORUS A convex moulding of semicircular section – especially at the base of a column.

TORUS MOULDING Large half-round convex moulding. ⟶ **SCOTIA MOULDING**

TOURBILLON MOVEMENT A watch movement designed to compensate for the fact that a watch keeps different times according to the position in which it is held, by revolving completely once every minute and thus averaging out errors.

TOURMALINE ⟶ **STONES**

TOWER POUND ⟶ **WEIGHTS**

TRAIN In a clock or watch, a set of wheels and pinions gearing with each other to drive either the hands (the '**GOING TRAIN**') or the striking mechanism (the '**STRIKING TRAIN**').

TRANSFER PRINTING A means by which decoration, mass-produced by a printing process, is transferred to pottery.

TRAP-CUT ⟶ **GEM CUTS**

TRAVELLING CLOCK ⟶ **CLOCKS**

TREEN Made from a tree, wooden, and hence applied as a generic word to wooden domestic vessels, particularly bowls.

TREMBLANT Shaking; used particularly of a stone so set in the centre of a piece of jewellery that it can move.

TRENCHER A flat piece of wood, square or circular, on which food was cut up or served; hence a plate or platter.

TRIFID Split into three by deep clefts or notches.

TRIGRAM ⟶ **CHINESE TERMS**

TRIPOLI A fine earth from the place of the same name used as a polishing powder, especially for **GLASS**. Also called **ROTTEN-STONE**.

TRIPTYCH A set of paintings or carvings on three panels so hinged that the outer two fold over, and cover, the central one. Especially used as an altar-piece. ⟶ **DIPTYCH**, **POLYPTYCH**

TRITON From classical mythology, a being represented by a bearded man with the hindquarters of a fish (cf. mermaid).

TRIVET Originally a three-legged stand on which to place a pot or kettle before a fire, now frequently a bracket attaching to the top fire-bar of an open grate for the same purpose.

TROMPE L'OEIL A technique in painting and painted decoration, making use of perspective and foreshortening, to deceive the eye into mistaking the apparent for the real.

TROPHY An ornamental or symbolic group of arms and similar military spoils, originally commemorative of a victory in battle.

TROY ⟶ **WEIGHTS**

TSUBA Oval metal guard of a Japanese sword; frequently decorated with very fine artistry, including inlays of precious metals or gem stones.

TS'UNG ⟶ **CHINESE TERMS**

TULIP-WOOD ⟶ **WOODS**

TUMBLER (1) The flat-based cylindrical drinking glass that now sits so firmly on the table started life as a cup with a round or pointed base that could not be set down until it had been emptied. This makes its name more logical and explains the residual taper to-day. It was often of silver or gold.

(2) Within a lock, a spring-held piece, whose projection must be lifted from the notch in the bolt by a key before the bolt can be moved.

TUREEN   A deep, generally oval vessel, originally of **EARTHEN-WARE** (whence the name for it was first spelled **TERRINE**), now often of **PLATE**, with a lid, from which soup is served. Also, a smaller vessel of similar shape, for serving sauce or gravy.

TURQUOISE ⟶ **STONES**

TUSCAN ⟶ **ORDER**

TUTENAG ⟶ **ALLOY**

TYG   A cheeky little word of quite unknown parentage, attributed to the seventeenth and eighteenth centuries, meaning a drinking cup with two or more handles. If you must reject the quaint, you may spell it **TIG**.

TYGER WARE ⟶ **TIGER WARE**

U   **UNDERGLAZE BLUE** ⟶ **CERAMIC COLOURS**

V   **VANDYKE**   Vandyke (who died in 1641) painted portraits of people wearing collars of lace or linen with a deep-cut edge. So to-day a Vandyke is a notched, deeply indented, or zigzag border or edging, and also one of a number of deep-cut points on the border of a garment.

VARGUEÑO   A Spanish piece of furniture, a cabinet on a stand, generally of plain wood, characteristically walnut, decorated with metal plates, having a drop-leaf front and numerous small drawers within.

VASELINE WARE   A **GLASS** similar to **CARNIVAL GLASS** of thick texture and a colour resembling that of vaseline.

VELLUM   A fine kind of **PARCHMENT**, prepared from the skins of calves, lambs, or kids for writing, painting, or binding.

VELVET ⟶ **TEXTILES**

VELVETEEN ⟶ **TEXTILES**

VENEER   Very thin board of precious or elegant wood glued to surface of a plain or cheaper wood to produce decorative effect at reduced cost in material.

VERDE DI PRATO MARBLE ⟶ **STONES**

VERGE   A long spindle provided with two **PALLETS** that are alternately moved by the **SCAPEWHEEL** in a verge escapement.

VERMEIL   The French term for **SILVER-GILT**.

VERNIS MARTIN   A varnish, invented about 1730 by two French brothers named Martin, derived from gum copal, to imitate oriental lacquer. Used on furniture, panelling, small boxes, etc.

VERRE EGLOMISÉ   Flat glass that is decorated by having laid behind it gold or silver foil engraved with a pointed tool. The name derives from a French picture-framer, Glomy, of the eighteenth century, though the technique goes back to Roman times.

VERT ⟶ **HERALDIC TERMS**

VESICA   A pointed oval figure, bounded by parts of two equal circles passing through each other at their centres, used as an architectural motif or an aureole to enclose devotional statues, etc.

VESTMENT   Any garment, but particularly any of the various robes used in religious and similar ceremonies, frequently collected for the richness or beauty of their embroidered decoration. In the Christian church a full-length neck-high plain dark cassock is covered by a half-length plain white surplice or alb, and the richer vestments are worn over these. Some of these are:

   CHASUBLE   A   sleeveless   mantle   covering   body   and shoulders worn over the alb and stole by the celebrant of the Mass or Eucharist.

COPE   A long cloak made of a semi-circular piece of cloth.

MITRE   The tall hat of a bishop, deeply cleft at the top, and having front and back surfaces in the shape of a pointed arch.

STOLE   A narrow strip of silk or linen worn round the neck, the ends hanging down straight or crossed in front.

VIGNETTE   (1) A decorative design on a blank space in a book, unenclosed, and especially having the edges shading off into the surrounding paper.

(2) A photographic portrait of head and shoulders with the edges shading off into the background.

VINAIGRETTE   A small ornamental box or bottle, generally with a sponge soaked with aromatic or pungent salts. ⟶ **POMANDER, POUNCET-BOX**

VIOLETWOOD ⟶ **WOODS**

VITRINE   A glass-fronted display case.

VITRUVIAN SCROLL   A convoluted scroll pattern used as an ornament, named after (as Americans would say, for) a Roman architect of the first century B.C., one Marcus Vitruvius Pollio. Said to resemble stylized wares, it is also known as the Greek ware-pattern.

VOIDER   A tray or basket in which dirty dishes and fragments of food are placed when clearing a food table.

VOLUTE   A spiral scroll, such as that forming the chief ornament in the capital of an Ionic column⟶ **ORDER**. Applied to the scrolled end of a chair arm.

VOLVELLE   A device of movable circles surrounded by other, graduated circles, to calculate rising and setting of sun and moon, high and low tides, etc. Of a clock, a subsidiary face showing, for example, the phases of the moon.

W **WAITER**   In addition to man-servant can mean a **SALVER** or small tray.

WALL CLOCK ⟶ **CLOCKS**

WALNUT ⟶ **WOODS**

WASH   In water-colour painting a broad thin layer of colour laid on by a continuous movement of the brush.

WASTER ⟶ **CERAMICS**

WATER-GILDING   The process of applying gold to metal surfaces in the form of a liquid amalgam of gold and mercury, the mercury being driven off by evaporation. The process is called water-gilding because of the liquid form in which the gold is applied. It is also called fire-gilding because of the heat used to evaporate the mercury. The gold so applied may subsequently be **BURNISH**ed to mirror-gloss.

WEIGHTS   Tradition is not to be spurned or lightly set aside; and, when set aside, it is not always wise that it should be forgotten. This thought is appropriate to English systems of weight, where various tables exist, or have existed, and have left their mark on society and language. As Britain moves into Europe it seems that the metric system will gradually take over from the old British systems, as it already has in scientific work. But old things will still be referred to by old names, which must therefore needs be known. The British starting point is the Troy grain.

The **TOWER POUND** (or **SAXON MONEYER'S POUND**) of 5400 grains Troy existed until 1527, to give the weight of silver that must be contained in the coinage. This pound of silver was a pound of money; but it was sub-divided into 1½ marks. Although the mark has long disappeared in English money, the tradition has lingered on, for at Oxford and Cambridge fines imposed by the Proctors, the university police, for minor misdemeanours were, until the decimalization of the currency, 6 shillings and 8 pence (½ mark) and 13 shillings and 4 pence (1 mark). With a touching acknowledgement of supposed scales of wealth these were the fines respectively on the undergraduate and the graduate.

The Tower Pound was replaced by the **TROY POUND** of

5760 grains Troy. Troy apparently derived from a weight used at the fair of Troyes in France.

This was replaced, for all statutory purposes except weighing precious metals and stones, in 1878, by the older **AVOIRDUPOIS POUND** of 7000 grains Troy. So, when a piece of silver at sale is described as of so many ounces, they are (or should be) Troy ounces; but cheese is weighed in Avoirdupois ounces.

Gold, with its special mystique, has its own special nomenclature for the division of the Troy ounce.

The **METRIC SYSTEM** revolves around the **GRAM**, the weight of 1 cubic centimetre of distilled water, weighed in a vacuum at sea level. The relationship of these scales to one another, and the names of their sub-divisions are set out in Table VII, where Apothecaries' weight, used for compounding medicines, is thrown in for good measure.

WELLINGTON CHEST   A tall narrow chest of drawers (usually some six or seven), primarily for keeping papers, having a locking hinged flange down one side which keeps all the drawers in place. It dates from the early nineteenth century.

WHAT-NOT   Small rectangular stand with shelves, designed to stand against a wall for the display of ornaments, curiosities, etc. The term came into use about 1810.

WHEEL ENGRAVING   Engraving of glass and **HARDSTONES** with small treadle-driven copper wheels furnished with an abrasive.

WHEEL-LOCK   A **GUN-LOCK** in which the powder was fired by a spark produced by the friction of a small wheel against a piece of iron pyrites.

WHITE GOLD $\longrightarrow$ **ALLOY**

WILLOW WOOD $\longrightarrow$ **WOODS**

WOODBLOCK PRINT $\longrightarrow$ **PRINT**

WOODS   There can hardly be any wood that man has not used for his art or artefacts somewhere in the world. It would be as impossible as undesirable to list them all. The list that follows is no more than an indication of some of the characteristics of the woods employed in the commoner articles – furniture in particular – of interest to collectors. It is in any case to be remembered that most woods can be, and many are, dyed or stained. This is particularly the case with VENEER woods obtained from fruit trees (apple, etc.) when used in MARQUETRY, so that even a reference to colour in the list below is at best indicative only of that most frequently met. In furniture it is an observed curiosity that wood from fruiting trees (e.g. walnut, oak, pine, beech) is, regardless of whether it is soft (e.g. pine) or hard (e.g. oak and beech), more susceptible to the ravages of woodworm than are the non-fruiting woods.

ASH   A hard white wood, non-splintering, of straight grain, and much used in handles for tools.

CALAMANDER   A hard wood resembling ebony, from India and Ceylon. Yellowish brown with black mottling. A corruption of Coromandel, the name of a part of the Indian coast.

CAMPHOR WOOD   A heavy close-grained wood with a pleasant natural scent. Much used in the Orient for clothes chests, because its scent is insect-repellent.

DEAL   A generic name for the soft woods of the pine family, much used, apart from building, for the less visible parts (e.g. drawer linings) of cheaper furniture, or as the foundation on which costlier and more elegant VENEERS of other woods are glued.

EBONY   A close-grained, hard, very heavy tropical wood, its colouring being black with streaks of browny-grey. Extensively used for carving. Intrusive streaks of the lighter shade can be successfully concealed with black boot polish.

ELM   A heavy plain close-grained wood, little used in furniture making. But in its day much in demand for stalls in stables owing to its characteristic of not splintering.

HAREWOOD   SYCAMORE stained greenish-grey and used for VENEERS and in MARQUETRY.

HOLLY A hard almost white wood, used mainly to provide colour contrast in **MARQUETRY** and **CROSS-BANDING**.

KINGWOOD A Brazilian species of wood, probably from a *Dalbergia*, dark brown with a satiny sheen. ⟶ **VIOLET-WOOD**

LIGNUM VITAE A very hard brown or greenish-black wood from South America used for objects subject to hard wear.

LIME (LINDEN) The wood of the linden or lime tree, soft, finely textured, and without marked grain, is especially prized for carving, since it does not split when the chisel is used on it. White when first cut. Much used for the carving in **BAROQUE** churches of South Germany and Austria.

MAHOGANY A heavy tropical hardwood of close grain, and often of very beautiful figuring.

OAK A hard heavy wood, its grain often enlightened by figuring, very widely used for furniture.

PADOUK (WOOD) The wood, resembling **ROSEWOOD**, of a Burmese tree, of which Padouk is the native Burmese name.

PALISANDER = **ROSEWOOD**

PERNAMBUCO WOOD A South American wood used for making bows for violins.

PURPLEWOOD A close-grained wood, purple in tone, and with very little figure.

SABICU A Cuban wood, used from the early eighteenth century as a substitute for **MAHOGANY**, which it resembles.

SANDAL WOOD A naturally scented white, yellow, or red wood of tropical origin; usually used for smaller artefacts (boxes etc.) which, being closed, preserve something of the scent.

SATINWOOD Rich golden yellow wood used for veneers, inlays, etc.

SPANISH MAHOGANY **MAHOGANY** not from Spain at all, of course, but up to the middle of the nineteenth century from the Spanish colonies in tropical Central America.

Sometimes also, for the same reason, called **CUBAN MAHOGANY**, when the provenance was specific.

SYCAMORE   A white wood, which takes stain well.

TULIP-WOOD   A light ornamental wood, from the tulip-tree, used by cabinet makers. More loosely, the term is applied to a variety of coloured and striped woods.

VIOLETWOOD   A hard close-grained wood, purple in colour with darker streaks. Since the nineteenth century known in England as **KINGWOOD**.

WALNUT   The light brown wood of the nut tree of the same name, much used in furniture, generally as a veneer. Frequently very finely figured; sections cut from the root end of the trunk may be marked with small discs of a darker hue than the surrounding wood and this is known as **BURR** walnut. Solid walnut is much favoured for the stocks of sporting guns and rifles.

WILLOW WOOD   Apart from cricket bats willow wood has a rather exotic use, in the form of wheels on a lathe, for polishing the facets of cut glass.

YEW   Famous as the wood of the bows of the English long-bowmen, it is now used, mostly as a veneer, of pale yellow colour, in furniture.

WORSTED   A closely twisted yarn made of long-staple wool in which the fibres have been combed to lie parallel to each other; whence a woollen fabric woven from such yarn.

WU TS'AI ⟶ **CHINESE TERMS**

WYVERN ⟶ **HERALDIC TERMS**

YEW ⟶ **WOODS**

YING CHING ⟶ **CHINESE TERMS**

YU ⟶ **CHINESE TERMS**

YUEH-YAO ⟶ **CHINESE TERMS**

Z **ZARF** A container, shaped like an egg-cup, used in Turkey and elsewhere in the Middle East, for a small handleless coffee cup.

ZECCHINO $\longrightarrow$ **SEQUIN**

ZIRCON $\longrightarrow$ **STONES**

ZIRCON CUT $\longrightarrow$ **GEM CUTS**

Tables

For comparison with the information in TABLE II, the terminology and sizes (in inches) are the following

Emperor	72	× 48
Antiquarian	53	× 31
Double Elephant	40	× 26¾
Grand Eagle	42	× 28¾
Atlas	34	× 26
Colombier	34½	× 23½
Imperial	30	× 22
Elephant	28	× 23
Cartridge	26	× 21
Super Royal	27	× 19
Royal	24	× 19
Medium	22	× 17½
Large Post	21	× 16½
Copy or draft	20	× 16
Demy	20	× 15½
Post	19	× 15¼
Pinched Post	18½	× 14¾
Foolscap	17	× 13½
Sheet and ⅓ Foolscap	22	× 13½
Sheet and ½ Foolscap	24½	× 13½
Double Foolscap	26½	× 16½
Double Post	30½	× 19
Double Large Post	33	× 21
Double Demy	31	× 20
Brief	16½	× 13¼
Pott	15	× 12½

TABLE II *Printing paper sizes*

The names and sizes (in inches) of sheets of printing paper are as follows

Foolscap	17	× 13½
Double Foolscap	27	× 17
Crown	20	× 15
Double Crown	30	× 20
Quad Crown	40	× 30
Double Quad Crown	60	× 40
Post	19¼	× 15½
Double Post	31½	× 19½
Double Large Post	33	× 21
Sheet and ½ Post	23½	× 19½
Demy	22½	× 17½
Double Demy	35	× 22½
Quad Demy	45	× 35
Music Demy	20	× 15½
Medium	23	× 18
Royal	25	× 20
Super Royal	27½	× 20½
Elephant	28	× 23
Imperial	30	× 22

Table III · 111

TABLE III *Bound book sizes*

Resulting from the use of the sizes of paper given in TABLE II the size (in inches) and nomenclature of bound books are as follows

Demy 16mo	$5\frac{5}{8} \times 4\frac{3}{8}$
Demy 18mo	$5\frac{3}{4} \times 3\frac{3}{4}$
Foolscap Octavo (8vo)	$6\frac{3}{4} \times 4\frac{1}{4}$
Crown 8vo	$7\frac{1}{2} \times 5$
Large Crown 8vo	$8 \times 5\frac{1}{4}$
Demy 8vo	$8\frac{3}{4} \times 5\frac{5}{8}$
Medium 8vo	$9\frac{1}{2} \times 6$
Royal 8vo	$10 \times 6\frac{1}{4}$
Super Royal 8vo	$10\frac{1}{4} \times 6\frac{7}{8}$
Imperial 8vo	$11 \times 7\frac{1}{2}$
Foolscap Quarto (4to)	$8\frac{1}{2} \times 6\frac{3}{4}$
Crown 4to	$10 \times 7\frac{1}{2}$
Demy 4to	$11\frac{1}{4} \times 8\frac{3}{4}$
Royal 4to	$12\frac{1}{2} \times 10$
Imperial 4to	15×11
Crown Folio	15×10
Demy Folio	$17\frac{1}{2} \times 11\frac{1}{4}$
Royal Folio	$20 \times 12\frac{1}{2}$
Music	$14 \times 10\frac{1}{4}$

TABLE IV *Hardness of stones*

An Austrian gemmologist named Mohs devised a scale ranging from 1 to 10 for measuring the hardness of stones. His reference points are italicized in the table below, which includes a number of those mentioned in the entry under **STONES**.

Talc	1
Gipsum	2
Amber	2½
Calcite	3
Malachite	3½–4
Fluorite	4
Apatite	5
Opal	5½–6½
Rhodonite	5½–6½
Feldspar	6
Peridot	6½–7
Quartz	7
Tourmaline	7
Zircon	7½
Topaz	8
Spinel	8
Chrysoberyl cat's eye	8½
Corundum	9
Ruby	9
Diamond	10

Table V · 113

TABLE V *Scripts*

This is copperplate

This is cursive

𝕿𝖍𝖎𝖘 𝖎𝖘 𝖌𝖔𝖙𝖍𝖎𝖈

This is italic

This is roman

Within each category there is wide variety in the design of letters in each typeface or fount.

TABLE VI *Type sizes*

In any given typeface there are numerous sizes of type, each with its own name. In the typeface of this volume the names are illustrated thus

2-line pica	Typecas
2-line small pica	Typecasti
Paragon	Typecastin
Great primer	Typecasting
2-line brevier	Typecasting a
English	Typecasting an
Pica	Typecasting and c
Small pica	Typecasting and co
	Typecasting and com
Long primer	Typecasting and comp
	Typecasting and comp
Bourgeois	Typecasting and compo
	Typecasting and composi
Brevier	Typecasting and composi
Minion	Typecasting and composing
Nonpareil	Typecasting and composing m
Agate	Typecasting and composing mac
Ruby	Typecasting and composing mach
Five-point Pearl	Typecasting and composing machin

Table VII · 115

TABLE VII *Weights*

TOWER WEIGHT

	Value					Troy equivalent		Metric equivalent	
[1 lb,	20	s	1½ marks	240 dwt		5400	gr	322.3	gm
called Troy]	13⅓ s	1	mark	160 dwt		3600	gr	214.8	gm
	1	s		12 dwt		370	gr	16.1	gm
				1 dwt		22.5 gr		1.34	gm

TROY WEIGHT

[1 lb Troy]	12 oz Troy	240 dwt Troy		5760 gr	373.2	gm
	1 oz Troy	20 dwt Troy		480 gr	31.1	gm
		1 dwt Troy		24 gr	1.56	gm

AVOIRDUPOIS WEIGHT

1 lb Av.	16 oz Av.	256 drams Av.	7000	gr	453.6 gm
	1 oz Av.	16 drams Av.	437.5	gr	28.35 gm
		1 dram Av.	27.34 gr		1.74 gm

CARAT WEIGHT for gold and precious stones

1 oz Troy	24 carats (gold)	96 carat grains	480 gr
	1 carat (gold)	4 carat grains	20 gr

APOTHECARIES' WEIGHT

20 grains   = 1 scruple
 3 scruples = 1 drachm
 8 drachms = 1 ounce
The Apothecaries' grain is the Avoirdupois grain and the Apothecaries' ounce is the Troy ounce, of 480 grains.

METRIC WEIGHT

1 gram 15.432 Troy grains

lb = pound   oz = ounce   dwt = pennyweight   s = shilling
gm = gram   gr = grain

TABLE VIII *Chinese Dynasties*

Hsia 夏		2205–1766 BC
Shang 商		1766–1122 BC
Chou 周		1122– 256 BC
(Period of the Spring and Autumn		
Annals 春 秋		770– 481 BC)
(Period of the Warring States 戰 國		480– 222 BC)
Ch'in 秦		221– 207 BC
Han 漢		206 BC–AD 219
Three Kingdoms 三 國		AD 220–280
Wei 魏		220–265
Shu Han 蜀 漢		221–263
Chin 晉		265–420
Western Chin 西 晉		265–316
Eastern Chin 東 晉		317–420
Six Dynasties 六 朝		222–589

(A name referring to the dynasties which had their capitals on the site of the present Nanking: Tung Wu, Eastern Chin, Sung, Ch'i, Liang, and Ch'en)

Northern and Southern Dynasties	386–589
Northern Dynasties	386–581
Sui 隋	589–618
T'ang 唐	618–906
Five Dynasties 五 代	907–960
Sung 宋	960–1279
Northern Sung 北 宋	960–1127
Southern Sung 南 宋	1127–1279
Yuan 元	1280–1368

Ming Dynasty

Hung Wu	洪 武	1368–98
Chien Wen	建 文	1399–1402
Yung Lo	永 樂	1403–24
Hung Hsi	洪 熙	1425
Hsuan Te	宣 德	1426–35
Cheng T'ung	正 統	1436–49
Ching T'ai	景 泰	1450–6
T'ien Shun	天 順	1457–64
Ch'eng Hua	成 化	1465–87
Hung Chih	弘 治	1488–1505

Table VIII · 117

Cheng Te	正 德	1506–21
Chia Ching	嘉 靖	1522–66
Lung Ch'ing	隆 慶	1567–72
Wan Li	萬 曆	1573–1620
T'ai Ch'ang	泰 昌	1620
T'ien Ch'i	天 啟	1621–7
Ch'ung Cheng	崇 禎	1628–44

Ch'ing Dynasty

Shun Chih	順 治	1644–61
K'ang Hsi	康 熙	1662–1722
Yung Cheng	雍 正	1723–35
Ch'ien Lung	乾 隆	1736–96
Chia Ch'ing	嘉 慶	1796–1820
Tao Kuang	道 光	1821–50
Hsien Feng	咸 豐	1851–61
T'ung Chih	同 治	1862–74
Kuang Hsu	光 緒	1875–1908
Hsuan T'ung	宣 統	1909–12

TABLE IX *Hallmarks (Silver) – some illustrative punches*

Quality marks

Sterling	England	Lion passant	[punch] 1545	[punch] 1551	[punch] 1975
	Scotland	Thistle	[punch] 1956–68		
	Ireland	Hibernia	[punch] 1839		
Britannia [Compulsory 1696–1720]	England	Britannia	[punch] pre 1975		

Town marks

London	Leopard's head	[punch] 1896–1915	[punch] 1916–1932	[punch] 1936–on
	Lion's head erased (Britannia standard)	[punch] 1697–8	[punch] 1716–19	
Birmingham	Anchor	[punch] 1773–97	[punch] 1798–1823	
Sheffield	Crown; from 1975 rose	[punch] 1823	[punch] 1975	
Edinburgh	Castle	[punch] 1747–54	[punch] 1806–8	
Dublin	Crowned Harp	[punch] 1821	[punch] 1829	
Chester (closed 1962)	Sword and 3 sheaves	[punch] 1680	[punch] 1784–96	
Glasgow (closed 1964)	Tree with bird, bell, and fish	[punch] 1819	[punch] 1871–96	
Exeter (closed 1882)	Till 1701 an X with a crown in a circle; thereafter a three-towered castle	[punch] 1675	[punch] 1721	
Newcastle (closed 1883)	three separate castles	[punch] 1759–78	[punch] 1800–14	
Norwich (closed 1701)	Castle surmounting a lion; later a seeded rose crowned; later a rose with a stem.	[punch] 1568	[punch] c.1620	[punch] c.1675
York (closed 1856)	Till 1700 half fleur-de-lis and half leopard head; thereafter cross with five lions passant.	[punch] 1568	[punch] 1787–1811	

Table IX · 119

Duty marks

1784–5	🖼
1786–1820	🖼
1821–33	🖼
1834–7	🖼
1838–90	🖼

Commemorative marks

1933–4–5	King George V's Jubilee	🖼
1952–3	Queen Elizabeth's Coronation	🖼
1977	Queen Elizabeth's Jubilee	🖼